RISE UP &
WALK!

A JOURNEY TO HEALING

RISE UP & WALK!

A JOURNEY TO HEALING

Rachel Wilfong

WINEPRESS WP PUBLISHING

ISBN 1-57921-197-6
Library of Congress Catalog Card Number: 99-63453

Endorsements

Reading *Rise Up and Walk!* has helped me as a mother and grandmother to meet the spiritual challenges of those rolls. My admiration for Rachel grew as I read how she displayed spiritual strength and faith in God in difficult times. In reading her description of her Sunday school class, and how it developed and grew, I was encouraged to see the potential for growth in our church. Her Spirit-inspired, wisdom-filled words will be a guide to many Christians and non-Christians alike.

—Carolyn Grant, kindergarten teacher and church leader

I have always believed in miracles, but never personally experienced one up close. To have Rachel return to the clinic enjoying life without pain and muscle weakness was a blessing to me. As her Muscular Dystrophy Association therapist, I could not discount the change in Rachel's functional skills and muscle strength. As I read the last chapter of *Rise Up and Walk! . . . a Journey to Healing,* I started my own

emotional and spiritual healing journey. Thank you Rachel, for believing in miracles and sharing your story with me.
—Tina Abate, PT
St. Francis Center for Health and Rehabilitation
Cape Girardeau, Missouri

Rachel has been a patient of the St. Francis MDA Clinic for several years, and each time she returned for an evaluation she had become more debilitated. We were so surprised and pleased when Rachel returned to the clinic, walking without assistance and no longer in pain. It is truly a miracle.
—Debbie Drury BSN, RN, CRRN.
Clinic Nurse Coordinator
Kelso, Missouri

When Rachel and her husband, Merideth, came to our church, she was confined to a wheelchair. I remember helping her enter and exit the church building for services. You could see in her eyes, although she tried to hide it, that she was in great pain. The Sunday that Rachel first walked unaided through the doors of our church was a bona fide miracle - the greatest miracle I have ever witnessed! God answered her prayers. Rachel and her husband's undying faith in God and commitment to our church has truly touched my soul and given me hope and inspiration. I believe that the Lord led this couple to our church so that our little congregation could experience the hope that true faith provides. I hope that everyone who reads her story will be touched the way I was.
—Paul S. Wills, Ph.D.
Coop Fisheries Research Lab, SIUC, Carbondale, Illinois

Acknowledgements

Many people have encouraged me to write this book. First Baptist Church family at Hope, Indiana, stood by me and prayed for my healing while I struggled with muscular dystrophy. I thank the Good News Sunday School class members who physically carried me up and down steps so that I could continue to teach them. The entire church family celebrated my healing in 1997. As they had encouraged me on my journey to healing, they gave me the courage and determination to tell my story.

A very special person who deserves recognition is my husband, Merideth. He provided me everything I needed to write and never complained of the hours that I spent writing this book. When it appeared I would not be delivered from the wheelchair for a while, he encouraged me to refresh my skills in writing and begin work for publication. After I gave up driving, he made arrangements to see that I kept my appointments. The distance did not matter to him. Since the time I began putting this material together, he has been by my side to make sure the book was published. I thank him for his faithfulness. Without him, you would not be reading this.

It takes many people to write a book: family, friends, and caring publishers like Athena and Chuck Dean with their able editing staff. I do thank you for selecting to share in my journey to healing. My desire is that you will be encouraged to walk in faith and in the love of our Lord Jesus Christ.

Contents

Foreword

A story of healing as dramatic as that of Rachel Wilfong's deserves telling to let the world know that God still heals today. Those who have known Rachel through the past twenty years can have no doubt that a tremendous miracle has taken place. They have witnessed what the debilitating disease of Polymyalgia Rheumatica can do to a physical body. They have also seen what God can do by observing that He instantaneously touched her body. After almost twenty years, including fifteen confined to a wheelchair, she was able to get up and walk with energy and strength.

What my wife will not tell you, I want to share. You can better appreciate the following testimony if you know how she suffered great pain, as well as physical limitation, with great patience and courage. Few people knew how much pain she endured, because she never complained. I never saw her despondent or lacking in faith. Her faith in God remained super strong, and she continued to serve the Lord. She was always faithful in church and taught an adult Sunday school class for a number of years. She started the class and built it up until eventually it was divided into two classes. Many of the present leaders in that church were won to the Lord and received their training in her class.

Whether in the wheelchair or on her feet, "Rae" has lived by a motto that we learned in Vacation Bible School the first year of our marriage: "I will do the best I can with what I have for Jesus' sake today."

Merideth E. Wilfong, Th.D.

Introduction

"There goes Rachel Wilfong walking down the street! I've never seen her walk before!"

My neighbor interrupted her telephone conversation with her friend. What she didn't know was that an amazing miracle had taken place in my home the night before. Fifteen years with Muscular Dystrophy was my physical bondage, but my healing for which many had been praying happened that night.

Since my diagnosis, I was confident that I would not spend the rest of my life in a wheelchair. A few days before the healing, my doctors informed me that there was nothing more they could do for me. Extremely troubled, I sought healing as never before. Was I really going to be delivered from that wheelchair? Why was it taking so long?

God spoke to my needs through a TV minister. Like many who pray for healing miracles, I was focusing upon my hurting body and a healing experience. I should look beyond the healing to the healer. When the invitation was given, I called out to Jesus. I gave Him fifteen years of bondage in a wheelchair and all of my durable equipment. In my broken spirit I asked Him to please heal me and fell gently back into my chair. Now, I know what "peace that passes understanding" means. My burdens were lifted, and healing came. I have tried to share in this book how personal Jesus was to me during my disability. He directed me in my journey to healing before I could write *Rise Up and Walk!*

1
When Disability Strikes

"Susan never meant to be mischievous," her sister-in-law, Helen, told me. "But she did funny little things. I remember when her son Lloyd was about three years old. He kept slipping off to his grandparents' house. She had retrieved him for the last time. With one arm tightly locked around his squirming body, she headed for the back lawn. She reached for a six-foot dog leash hanging on a post, and tied one end to the clothesline and the other to Lloyd's waist. 'If this works for the dog, it will work for you.' With that she simply went back and resumed her domestic chores, keeping a watchful eye on the lad as he paced back and forth from the end of the clothesline to the other."

Susan was a member of our church, confined to a wheelchair. She lived just outside our town at Miller's Merry Manor Convalescent Center. Her recent death had flooded my mind with reflections of her life, but I was curious about the type of person she was before her confinement. Helen seemed to be the one person most likely to satisfy my curiosity.

From where Susan sat, she had been an inspiration to me. Her cheerfulness and enthusiasm over God's creation, her patience in her suffering, her genuine compassion for others, and her cooperation with those who took care of her started a complete change in my life's direction.

Dear, sweet Susan! Not even her bony little fingers could obey her mind's commands. Her crippled, frail body crouched in her wheelchair. Her head was adorned with finger-sized waves, and every gray hair was in its place. It was always pulled tightly back over her ears, swirled into a smooth knot on the back of her head. Helen said that Clarence, Susan's husband, would never hear to let her have her hair cut.

"Susan had many talents," Helen continued. "She did her own sewing. I can never remember her when she was not wearing a blue or pink print or a checked dress. Whether the patterns were print designs with tiny flowers or soft checks, the collars and cuffs were trimmed with delicate, white lace. Only Susan's magic fingers could blind stitch that lace so perfectly."

Once Merideth and I visited Susan in her home before she moved to the health facility. Clarence went to the china cabinet, brought out one piece of chinaware after another, proudly showing us Susan's masterpieces. Each piece had been meticulously painted with designs of dainty flowers, mostly pink roses.

I learned that Susan had been an excellent cook. "She would never work in the field, not Susan," Helen said. "And you never, ever caught her in pants. I guess that was partly because of the way she was raised. She was a city girl, you know."

Helen said Susan loved talking on the phone with friends after she was unable to visit them in person. Her daughter would place the receiver in her bent, left hand. When it was secure, she would dial the number with her deformed right forefinger and talk for hours.

Just before Susan died, she asked to be taken back home. She wanted to spend her last days in her own home with her family.

"The family granted her that wish," Helen said as she fought back tears. "She had reserved pieces of her hand-painted china for each member of the family. As they came during those last days, she had them, one by one, take the piece reserved for them."

Helen stopped, sighed and tried to control her emotions. "I'll never forget when she gave me mine. She said, 'Helen, go to that little table by the china cabinet. You will find some-thing with your name on it. I want you to have it while I still live.' It was a beautiful plate, especially done for me. We each realize we have a part of Susan with us, along with our memo-ries of her."

In the fall of 1979, my husband and I were making our pastoral rounds at Miller's, the convalescent center. Our visit with Susan that day marked the beginning of an intense search in my life, one I never thought possible. We ap-proached the door to her room. She welcomed us with a twist of a smile. After we exchanged greetings, she gave her head a quick little jerk toward the nightstand.

"Clarence brought the flowers from our yard," she beamed.

It was not easy for Susan to form words as she talked about her two favorite subjects, Clarence and flowers. As she struggled to express her excitement over the beautiful arrange-ment, her blue eyes sparkled like diamonds.

"O Susan, they are so pretty." I commented. "And the pink roses are your favorites, aren't they?"

"My very favorite!" she replied.

"And look at that lovely orchid. I know that's out of Clarence's greenhouse, isn't it?" I could see she was pleased.

"Did you help Clarence pick the flowers, Susan?" my husband teased.

"Yes," she drawled with that twist of a smile again. "And I'm tired, too," she teased back.

It was her tiny, helpless fingers that my eyes fixed upon, starting flashbacks in my drifting mind. I remembered Helen's description of Susan when she was well. She was a bit heavyset, about one hundred and sixty pounds and a good five-feet-four-inches tall. I could see her in a light blue dress, the collar and cuffs trimmed in delicate white lace.

My mind shifted. I could see Susan holding Lloyd, the squirming, protesting three-year-old, as she carried him to the clothesline.

Then there was a beautiful wedding in progress, right before me. My eyes were focused on the pink, white, and blue flowers Susan had arranged for it.

What's this? There is a church balcony, and underneath it is Susan in a soft, pink checked dress. She is surrounded by a crowd of eager primary children, just as Helen described it. That's the makeshift Sunday School room where she taught for nearly fifteen years.

Then I heard the familiar voice of a friend in a sick room: "I can tell Susan's been here." Helen said Susan was always a step ahead of her when she visited a shut-in. She never wanted recognition for her deeds, but they could not be kept a secret. Evidence that she had been there was visual. A floral arrangement, a dish of food, and if she had no flowers, she created some with those magic fingers of hers. Another friend had said it was as though her spirit remained wherever she had been.

"Visiting time is up!" The voice of a nurse brought me out of the trance. "Time for this little lady to be helped into bed for her rest."

The kind nurse tenderly, and ever so carefully, lifted Susan's frail body into the bed. Although her body wreaked with pain, she never uttered a sound.

Questions began to bombard my mind. How could this terrible thing happen to such a sweet, God-loving, talented and useful person? How can she be so cheerful, so loving and patient and full of praise to her Lord?

She was handling herself well in her suffering. I wonder how I would do. Surely, I have not touched the surface in my ability to understand such things. And what about praying for others? How could I intelligently pray for Susan when I have never been where she's been?

Merideth and I moved up to Susan's bed to pray before we left her. While he prayed aloud, each of us carefully touching a crippled hand, I was praying my own prayer.

"Lord, how can I honestly, sincerely pray for Susan?" I prayed silently. "I don't understand any of this. 'Let this mind be in you which was also in Christ Jesus: Who, being in the form of God, thought it not robbery to be equal with God . . . .' I am to have the mind of Christ, and if I am to be like You, I will have the same love You have. Could you please just give me a portion of the love and compassion that Jesus had among the suffering crowds and that Susan has for You and others? Please create in me a new heart," I begged.

Remembering very little about our trip home, I noticed we had reached the parsonage. Deep troubling thoughts of Susan crowded my mind. I knew the prayer I had just prayed to God was already heard. He would, in time, respond with help. One thing I knew, my motives must changed. I must make sure I am not "just going along with my husband." Moments with shut-ins and the sick, as well as the whole, must be made from a caring heart, my caring heart. I must share God's love with them whatever their circumstances. Recognition for my deeds must not matter. As the friend had said about Susan, my deeds must be unselfish ones. Whatever it took for God to help me, I was committed to be clay in the potter's hand.

In November of that year something started happening to my body. There was a growing stiffness in my pelvis. Getting in and out of the car became more unbearable. Driving was a painful challenge. The pain of it all led me to see our family physician. When his treatment for tendonitis failed, he made appointments for me to see specialists. After frequent trips to doctors and hospital labs, a diagnosis was reached.

"Well, Mrs. Wilfong, you have a disease of the muscles called Polymyalgia Rheumatica," the doctor announced.

"Poly—my—a what?" I stuttered. "What in the world is that?"

"It is an attack on the large muscles, related to muscular dystrophy," he explained. "It's a rare disease, and very little is known about it."

"What can we do?" I shot back.

"We can treat it with a steroid," he said. "We must experiment. Each patient responds differently to therapy. If it works, we can keep the symptoms under control. That's all I can offer you. I'm sorry," he spoke regretfully.

"What about the future?" I asked him, a little afraid of the answer.

"Well," he said, "it doesn't get better. In fact, the disease progresses. However, a percentage of patients experience remission within two years. Let's hope you are one of those statistics."

Back home on my couch in the family room, so stiff that I could hardly move, I kept hearing the doctor's words. "It doesn't get better, in fact it progresses." I knew I was in trouble. I ventured the hope that I would be one of those who would experience remission.

I cried out to God. "What's happening to me? What will Merideth do with a disabled wife? Pastors' wives can't be immobile." I could see myself giving up all the important positions of leadership I had enjoyed for years in my church and denomination. "Who would take my place? Who would do my housework?" I wept as an avalanche of fearful questions crushed me.

"Oh dear God," I continued to pray. "Don't let this happen to me. Let the doctors be wrong. At least, let me be one of the few who goes into remission in a year or two. Let me not become a handicap."

At that moment it was as though I heard the voice of God. *"Do you remember the prayer you prayed when you were visiting Susan?"*

My heart answered, *"I remember."*

He continued, *"Well, this is how Susan felt at one time. You want a mind of compassion and understanding for those who are suffering. You will have a new mind and a new heart. You will be able to pray for them intelligently, with complete understanding and pure love. But you have to learn how. I will be with you,"* He promised.

"Oh yes, Susan. I almost forgot Susan, Lord. I must not forget the Susans of this world." I could hear my own voice speaking through uncontrollable weeping. Sobs shook my body. Warm tears flowed down my face. God was ever so near as I visualized many people in need. He had actually heard my prayer for compassion. Was He really going to give it to me?

"OK, Lord, I'll listen and learn from you," and I recommitted myself to Him.

At that instant I felt a peace that passes all understanding (Phil. 4:7). Frustration was gone. My heart began to praise God. He was so personal to me, so intimate. He was responding to my prayer, and I was aware of His holy perfectness. Then I knew why Susan was so pleasant. God was personal to her. She felt her worth in Him. Her disabilities had not controlled her life. I had so much to learn. I had just begun.

Lesson one as a disabled person was in the spring of 1982. For three years I had managed to walk with assistance. Merideth and I joined our church youth group in a "fun day" at King's Island near Cincinnati, Ohio. I refused to be labeled a "handicap." I insisted on dragging myself around throughout the day, declining a wheelchair. Just outside a theater near the end of the day, I collapsed on a park bench.

"Here it comes," I thought. *"I have to give in and use a wheelchair. I can walk no more!"*

I called out to my husband, "Honey, go ahead and rent me a wheelchair. I can go no further this way."

"Sure, Rae," he responded with a voice of relief. He had been waiting for those words all day.

It wasn't until I was nestled into the wheelchair that I realized how thoughtless I had been. I had put my husband and my friends through torture, all because of my pride. I wanted to cry, but I restrained myself. Never again would I be so self-centered. Susan would never have been so inconsiderate. I had been thinking only of myself. Such an attitude was unforgivable! My mind was made up. I would consider purchasing a wheelchair. There were several brochures tucked away in a file drawer. Merideth had brought them home for me to look at. Each time he suggested a wheelchair, I would put them aside and tell him I wasn't ready for that.

After that day at King's Island, we purchased a little AMIGO. This little three-wheel electronic wheelchair truly became my *amigo*, my friend. Soon after that, Merideth bought me a handicap van. A new exciting ministry for me had just begun.

In my resistance I had reminded myself of Lloyd, the three-year-old, who was tied to the clothesline. I'm sure Susan never released him until he had stopped resisting his confinement. Now that I no longer resisted the inevitable, I could relax and be content from where I sat. Resistance can only bring discomfort and frustration. Susan most certainly had known this for a long time.

God is not through with me yet, but from where I sit I know my motives are pure. I am learning the art of patience, the gift of love, and the virtue of caring and understanding which was reflected in Susan's life. One experience after another is now teaching me to be more like Christ, and Susan. Oftentimes at conferences and meetings in our travels I remember how Susan had to strain her neck to make eye contact with us. I am sure I have overlooked the difficulty of communication with those who were in wheelchairs when I was walking tall beside them.

There are many advantages from where I sit. Happy little faces of children touch mine as they hug me. I reach and touch them in response. Rather than stooping or squatting to make an imaginary seat, I've found matching their height is much easier in a wheelchair.

As they anticipate my response to them, our eyes meet. It's different from where I sit than when I stood equally tall with other adults. How often, and how many of those little children have tugged at my skirt to get my attention, only to leave disappointed because I was too busy talking with adults!

When I come face to face with other disabled persons, it is easy to take a moment to share with them. What a joy it is to visit someone in the hospital. While I can't stand over them sharing the joy of living, I can reflect Susan's spirit, which comes from knowing Christ, letting them know I understand. They know I didn't just "come along with my husband." Knowing I have been where they are, they are sure of my compassion for them.

There is no question about the struggles which started in Susan's room that day in 1979. If God could not get glory from the physical and spiritual changes, it would be unnecessary for Him to bother. The special ministry He has for me is being fulfilled because of His "tough love." Like a disciplined child, I nestle snugly into His comforting arms, gaining assurance that He cares enough for me to trust me to represent His Son to others. Now that I am sitting where Susan sat, I reclaim the motto which I adopted as a child in Vacation Bible School. "I will do the best I can with what I have for Jesus' sake today."

🌿 🌿 🌿 🌿 🌿

DENIAL

Much can be said about stages of denial through which people go. Pride had become my prison walls. How could I make myself surrender to a wheelchair? But I must, and I did. Once I passed this denial stage, I learned to accept help from others. Good things began to happen. One by one, my needs were met.

The little AMIGO wheelchair became my friend, gave me freedom and made my family happy. Kids? They loved it.

My thoughtful spouse, my enabler, was on a constant alert for ideas to make things more convenient for me. First, the wheelchair, then he located a van. A van equipped for my handicap was expensive. Help came from Indianapolis, the Muscular Dystrophy Association (MDA) and the owner of a durable equipment corporation. The owner, himself, had a disability. Out of care for others, he customized handicap vans and equipment for vehicles. Almost like magic, the little yellow handicap van with all the appropriate controls, including a lift, made its way into my drive. A toggle switch on the inside and outside allowed me to operate the lift, and I could drive the van myself. My denial was history.

The van with the lift added ease to our traveling together. I could go to the Grand Canyon, Yellowstone National Park, and all the way to Mexico in the van, but sometimes the wheelchair was not powerful enough for the rough terrain. After traveling a month out west and back to Indiana, I kissed the little three-wheel friend good-bye and replaced it with a Fortress Scientific 2000. The comparison of the two scooters was like comparing a Ford and a Cadillac. No incline was too steep for the Fortress, no sidewalk too rough to tackle, and the custom designed shoulder-and-head support was very comfortable. Only wet and rainy weather kept me indoors.

In my travels to meetings, conferences, and conventions, I have been physically carried up and down steps. I have mounted all kinds of ramps, and ridden various chair lifts, but in October of 1989 I had my first experience with a automated step climber. Here's what happened:

Arriving at a conference, I was transferred into this crazy, almost frightening unit that would carry me up and down three flights of steps. A gentleman carefully helped me into the chair and buckled me in as though he was preparing me for a space flight. Once I was securely buckled in, he pushed a button that started the unit and it slowly climbed the steps. Two things bothered me, however. First, I was forced to leave my trusted Fortress at the bottom of the steps. Second, I couldn't operate the stair climber by myself. Since I was scheduled to speak at the conference, it was fortunate that I made it to the top of the stairs where I could enter the sanctuary. Needless to say, with three flights between the sanctuary and the dining room, I had my ups and downs that day.

Someone, somewhere, seems to be working constantly on a new invention for the convenience and comfort of the physically challenged population. For those who are putting their ideas into action, I am grateful. They have provided me with a piece of equipment for every domestic chore, as well as all types of items for recreation, sports, and work.

People give of themselves. They give money for Jerry's Kids. The MDA accepted me as one of Jerry's elder kids in 1983. People give to various organizations to make life better for crippled children in various funds. They give to Easter Seals, to The American Heart Association, and many more organizations, all because they care for others. More and more thought is given each year to assist the physically challenged. I say "thanks" from where I sit.

Why the Wheelchair, Lord?

In March 1985 we celebrated the sixteenth birthday of our granddaughter, Deanette, who had been with us for two years. Reflecting upon those years, I remembered a statement I had made: "If I had a second chance to raise teenagers, I believe I could do a much better job than I did with our daughters."

Shortly after I confidently made that bold statement to a Sunday School class of young parents, Deanette came for what was supposed to be a summer visit. She had lived with us periodically in the past when she was small and had spent several weeks each summer with us. This time, however, she wanted to remain with us and complete high school. The following September she would be a freshman.

I recalled my bold statement and recanted, "Lord, I didn't mean what I said. I don't think I'm ready for four years of this at all!"

I considered my disability. Allowing Deanette to stay with us was not an easy decision. Nevertheless, negotiations began. With the consent of Deanette's father, whose marriage was unstable, she would make her home with us. We all wanted to be certain that her father's troubles would not interrupt her education. We agreed that joint custody between her mother and grandparents would be the best for her.

My husband and I continued to pray for the healing of my body. It was becoming apparent why I needed the wheelchair. I could be available for Deanette, to be there for her before and after school each day.

One afternoon the front door flew open and Deanette belted out, "I'm home!" I found myself praising God. The "second chance" He was giving me to be guardian over a teenager was a blessing. Accompanying the "I'm home" blast was a breath of fresh air from the door left ajar. The click of the refrigerator door, and the humming of its operation while Deanette tried to decide on a snack, let me know that she would be in my office soon.

God had given me a divine assignment to be available for my granddaughter, who had become my friend. Her interruptions were blessings. It was no inconvenience for me to put a writing project on hold while I listened to her describe her day in school. Before my disability, my roll in the life of the church and denomination had consumed most of my time. With that lifestyle, no one would be there for Deanette. She would have become a ward of the court and placed in a home with strangers. How could I live with that? Yes, God was in control of our lives.

I felt the Holy Spirit upon me. God had not enslaved me to a wheelchair. He had allowed me a special opportunity, a special freedom. My freedom does not depend upon any person or situation. I may use a wheelchair, but it cannot control me, nor can a muscle disease that put me there control me. I praised Him for delaying my healing. God has specially chosen me. He has assigned me to an opportunity of service I could handle from where I sit. "Why the wheelchair, Lord?" That is not the question.

"Now the Lord is the Spirit, and where the Spirit of the Lord is, there is freedom" (2 Cor. 3:17). I cannot comprehend God's great love for me through His Son, Jesus. His faithful presence to strengthen me, His guidance when I seek His will in my life, and His forgiveness when I miss the mark overwhelms me.

> Therefore we do not lose heart. Though outwardly we are wasting away, yet inwardly we are being renewed day by day. For our light and momentary troubles are achieving for us an eternal glory that far outweighs them all. So we fix our eyes not on what is seen, but on what is unseen. For what is seen is temporary, but what is unseen is eternal. (2 Cor. 4:16-18)

"Why not the wheelchair, Lord?" That is the question.

🌿 🌿 🌿 🌿 🌿

Hurdles, Obstacles and Life's Surprises!

The extent to which a hurdle becomes an obstacle depends upon the person's preparedness. A hurdle may be somewhat a surprise, however. With a life of practice and training, a minor stumble may be avoided. We are forever facing little surprises in our lives, which sometimes tend to alter our routine. However, with the Word of God to guide us, the Holy Spirit to empower us, and prayer to pull us through, we most certainly can overcome.

Occasionally my plans must be altered. An appointment must be rescheduled, a meal must be put on the back burner, or my husband may ask me to make a pastoral call with him. Rescheduling an appointment is simple. Sitting down to a late meal isn't so bad, but what about that pastoral call? Is my physical pain so much that I say no to an opportunity to witness in the name of Jesus? My priorities must be evaluated. Is it too much to expect that I should be spared the pain of getting into the van to represent my Lord to another person who is suffering? Should I be exempt from trials and temptations in my Christian walk? Jesus, the Son of God, was not spared pain and suffering. Commitments are easy to make and so easy to break. We can say it really doesn't matter and go on our way doing that which requires less effort.

A mother gave birth to her first baby. I remember her words as she held him, "My baby doesn't look right." She learned within hours that her son was born with only half of a heart. He lived through the delicate surgery necessary for him to survive. His little heart was repaired, and he was sent home with rigid medical instructions. Being good parents, they closely followed the instructions for administering special medications. They were told how important it was to give it on time and to never skip a dose. It would have been so easy for those parents to keep him home from church out of fear of infection. It would have been much more simple for them to give him his medicine at home.

I remember that they brought their little son, Bryan, to church on Sunday mornings, and returned for evening worship. The father set his watch to signal when it was time for Bryan's medicine. Once they were accustomed to the routine, they put him in the nursery with all the other children. They didn't let runny noses, coughs, and the possibility of contamination alter their commitment to their Lord. They kept their priorities straight. They were "seeking first the Kingdom of God and his righteousness" for their son. True, Bryan was exposed to possible contamination. But he also was exposed to an atmosphere of love that his church family could offer him. His parents never regretted bringing him to church, because they knew that his life was totally dependent upon God. Their confidence was in God. He would take care of their little family. Bryan's three years on earth exceeded more than was expected by the medical community. In those three years he demonstrated the blessings which came because of the wise choices his parents had made for him. In order for children to be blessed of God, parents must bring them to Him.

I have heard couples pray, asking God to bless them with a child. God gives and so quickly the gift is forgotten. So much more is given back to us when we expose them to beautiful experiences with God's family. Truly, it can be said of Bryan's parents, grandparents, aunts and uncles, that they have kept their faith and have dealt with this hurdle well. They have had the blessed comfort that they have given Bryan the "better" things in life, and no regrets can haunt his loving parents who have kept their priorities in order. Bryan's short life blessed them, God gave them another son shortly after Bryan's death. If you were to join this family, each one would share his or her own story of how Bryan's life and death strengthened them in the Lord.

I do not have a corner on coping with obstacles, hurdles, or life's little surprises, but I thank God that His grace is sufficient to help me stay true to Him.

❧ ❧ ❧ ❧ ❧

FAMILY REUNION (MY PITY PARTY)

One hot summer day in July my mother and a couple of my brothers left to attend the Chadwick Family Reunion in Missouri. Mother was so joyful that five of her six children would be there. As far as I know, she has never had us all together since we left home. Her excitement mounted as she talked of how anxious she was to see all of them.

Suddenly she said, "All of my children will be with me except you, Rae."

Until she made that remark, I was sharing Mother's joy. She would see three of her children whom she had not seen in several years. Knowing there was no way I could arrange to be with them, my heart began to feel sad.

I sat in my wheelchair in the doorway watching their departure, feeling left out. It had been a few years since I had seen my only sister, and longer than that since I last saw three brothers. Warm tears began to roll down my cheeks, and their automobile blurred as it backed out of the drive and onto the street. I pivoted my wheelchair around and closed the door.

"Facial tissue to the rescue," I thought. *"Time for a pity party!"* But what a waste! I knew my family would all be together by Saturday of that week. I fantasized. I could see all of them hugging and kissing. Yes, they were shedding tears of gladness. A big teardrop splashed onto my arm, reminding me of where I was and what I was doing.

It occurred to me that the reunion in Missouri was only temporary. My family in Missouri would be happy a short time. They would discuss their jobs, their children and grandchildren, and with their various health problems, health would be a topic of discussion. They would surely talk about how much medicine they were taking, comparing their ills and pills. It would be important to their conversation to talk about Rae's rare muscular diseases, the names of which none of them could pronounce, and about which they could only speculate.

My *pity party* turned into a quiet time with God. A sigh of relief came as I wiped away the teardrops which had splashed on my arm. Our earthly family reunion does not compare to that ultimate reunion when Jesus comes for His loved ones. What will we talk about then? We can't talk about our aches and pains. There won't be any. There will be no more arthritis, no heart disease, no family crisis, and no wheelchairs. I cannot imagine the joy that will be ours at that reunion. I suppose we'll fix our eyes on Jesus, Lord of Lord's. I will not be excluded from the ultimate reunion.

My *pity party* was short and soon forgotten when I focused upon the Lord and His invitation for me to enjoy my relationship with Him where I sat. In Him there is unspeakable joy. With such security, there is no appropriate time or place for me to feel sorry for myself. The abundant life I have here on earth leaves no room for pouting. God's Word takes on new meaning as I read:

> Do not let your hearts be troubled. Trust in God; trust also in me. In my Father's house are many rooms; if it were not so, I would have told you. I am going there to prepare a place for you. And if I go and prepare a place for you, I will come back and take you to be with me that you

also may be where I am. You know the way to the place where I am going. (John 14:1-4)

🍃 🍃 🍃 🍃 🍃

If I Had a Choice

The wheelchair was my friend for several years. When I had surgery on both wrists a few years ago, I asked myself. *"If I had the choice, which would I rather give up, my arms and hands or my legs and feet?"*

With this question in mind, I considered how immobile I was without the use of my hands. With my hands I can cook, sew, clean house, and turn the doorknob to let someone into my home. What good is it to walk to the table if you can't eat? What good is it to run for the door if you can't turn the knob to let someone in? The phone rings. How can you answer it if you can't lift the receiver? There are hundreds of little things these fingers of mine do with no thought of how they are going to do it. Picking up a book is never a problem. I just pick up a book!

It occurred to me that my priorities were misplaced. Is it possible that I was looking for something "big and wonderful" to do for God? Do I feel guilty or useless if I can't come up with something out of the ordinary through which I can prove to God my love and loyalty? How many opportunities of service have I missed because I was looking too hard for something spectacular?

The Apostle Paul said: "Make it your ambition to lead a quiet life, to mind your own business and to work with your hands, just as we told you, so that your daily life may win the respect of outsiders so that you will not be dependent on anybody" (I Thess. 4:11).

The text in a sermon I once heard said it best. "Whatever your hand finds to do, do it with all your might, for in the grave, where you are going, there is neither working nor planning nor knowledge nor wisdom" (Eccles. 9:10).

"I will praise you as long as I live, and in your name I will lift up my hands" (Ps. 63:4). "I want men everywhere to lift up holy hands in prayer, without anger or disputing" (I Tim. 2:8).

My desire is to be a good wife of noble character. It is a challenging goal, and I am sure I shall never perfectly reach it, but when I read Proverbs 31:20, I want to open up my arms to the poor and extend my hands to the needy. The surgery on my hands taught me to praise God for the little things. I will never feed myself without thanking God for my hands. The crafts I do with my hands are very little, but I will never take my hands for granted again.

🌿 🌿 🌿 🌿 🌿

Restrooms for Handicaps?

The most frequent question I am asked is, "What is your greatest obstacle with the wheelchair?" Well, I don't know about the greatest, but restrooms can be quite challenging when traveling. On par with the frustration of needing a restroom is locating one I can get into. The variety of architectural barriers is unlimited. There are small doorways, heavy doors, and bottlenecks inside and outside the facilities. Many of them have narrow passageways between the wall and the stalls.

While architectural design is not a specialty of mine, I have become very apt at figuring out how to get through some of the barriers. For example, the door of an alcove may swing open wide, but my wheelchair won't go all the way in.

I could leave the chair outside the alcove and close the door. But that leaves my purse and other personal belongings separated from me. I could place the front half of the chair in the alcove and let the door swing partially open to rest against it. Just about the time I think I've got it all figured out, I look up and discover that the exit door opens directly in front of me. I get the impression that a candid camera is invading my privacy. The only other choice I have is to leave.

Some restrooms are attractive and have the perfect alcove at the extreme end. It is usually designed so that the wheelchair can go all the way in, allowing the door to close. That, of course, is ideal! Or is it? After all, I have to get inside the larger area where the alcove is, don't I? Some of these doors weigh a ton.

A typical scene starts at the door. A kind lady rushes to help me get it open. She plants her feet solid in my path. When she realizes why I'm stuck in the doorway, she steps aside, makes a rainbow over me with her arms, determined to help me through. With my left hand holding the door, I finally persuade her to let go so I can move. So far, so good. I'm ready to hang a right when I notice a large trash can in the only space there is for me to turn if I am to reach the *perfectly-designed* alcove. The trash container is moved. I miss several pairs of feet as I carefully squeeze my chair through. Mission accomplished? Not quite! By the time I am ready to reverse the whole thing to exit, a new crew of ladies is lined up. The puzzled look on their faces shows that they have no idea how in the world I got in there in the first place. My frantic effort quickly alerts them that I must get out before they can move.

Then there are those restrooms at one of our favorite truck stop restaurants. Once I get past the cigarette, food, and candy machines, I should be able to ease on into the necessary room.

However, most of their doors are not only narrow, but also extremely heavy. The first step is to just move through them, where I find myself in a little passageway between the outer door and the inside of the restroom. Webster describes this little area as "a bodily cavity forming or suggesting an entrance to some other part." Ever since I got stuck in one of these *cavities* at a college in Indiana, I have always sent a scout to investigate the restroom, handicap sign or not.

Of course, I have learned not to take those signs seriously! I saw the following poem on a restroom wall:

> Most architectural barriers
> I've learned to take in stride—
> Those steps, those curbs, those revolving doors
> That make me stay inside.
> I can live with water fountains
> That are level with my ears;
> And I've not used a phone booth
> For these many, many years.
> But when it comes to restrooms
> It's really a pretty low blow;
> Knowing that when I've gotta,
> I ain't gonna get to go!
> I burn the rubber off my wheels,
> I can hardly wait—
> My chair is 30 inches,
> The John door is 28!
> Some plead for civil justice
> When they are sat upon,
> I ask for just one freedom—
> The right to use the John.
> I've thought about reforming
> And changing my evil ways,
> To be a model of deportment
> For the remainder of my days.

But then, when I get to Heaven
And sit before the Gate,
Will St. Peter say, "Sorry, you're 30 inches,
Our Pearly Gates are 28."

(MK—3/24/72)

❧ ❧ ❧ ❧ ❧

Cut Down to Size for Short Opportunities

What can one say in a letter to a cousin stricken with cancer, soon to die? If God opens a door of opportunity for ministry, He will match the minister to the size of it.

Did you ever stop to think how many *short* opportunities an average-sized adult misses? I have been in a unique physical position from which to share Jesus with others. Children come face-to-face with me to share exciting experiences they have. How convenient it is in my wheelchair to embrace a child, whisper encouraging and affectionate words in their ears. If I notice a toddler, who is not tall enough to reach me, some loving parent places the little one on my lap.

We don't always understand why we are allowed to suffer and undergo testing in life, but a few years ago I was standing tall (well, as tall as I could at 5' 2-1/2"). At least I was eye-to-eye with most adults.

I believed that someday I would walk again, but until then I bathed in the joy of being a child in a world of children. God allowed me to be confined to a wheelchair to learn. He wanted me to communicate with these little people. The average-sized person would seldom notice that my neck and shoulders were in pain when I had to look up at them. I've been up there with adults and overlooked the little people trying to get my attention. At the same time, I am sure I have overlooked adults who are sitting in wheelchairs. God has taught me how to pray for others who are confined in various ways, and how to love them and understand their feelings.

What if the little ones are curious or attracted to my wheels? I get into some powerful love action with them. They follow me in the mall. They ask me questions about my wheelchair. Often I have heard them ask their parents about my electronic scooter. "What is it?" they say. "Why is that lady riding in it?"

This gives me a unique opportunity to put them at ease as I attempt to satisfy their curiosity, especially when the parent cautions, "Don't bother the lady." Such a caution is often because of the parent's fears, not the child's.

Paul said, ". . . for I have learned to be content whatever the circumstances. I know what it is to be in need, and

"A new ministry began from where I sat," says Rachel, with a new wheelchair and van.

I know what it is to have plenty. I have learned the secret of being content in any and every situation, whether well fed or hungry, whether living in plenty or in want. I can do everything through him who gives me strength" (Phil. 4:11b-13).

I thank God for the unique position He has allowed me to be in. I am learning and growing. Learning of Him is most rewarding as I learn through His children, short or tall.

Muscular dystrophy cut Rachel "down to size," but her ministry to children improved.

🌿 🌿 🌿 🌿 🌿

RAMPS AND SUCH (TAKING CARE OF MYSELF!)

It happens over and over again! When a trip for the Wilfongs is in the planning stages, I always call months ahead to make reservations. I carefully explain that I operate a three-wheel wheelchair and I need certain types of facilities before I make a reservation.

In 1985 a hotel in Portland, Oregon, assured me that a room *accessible for handicaps* was reserved. When we arrived, we found the room on the ground floor. However, there was a step through the door into the room. My husband went on a search for some boards to serve as a ramp. He found some at a loading dock and the boards allowed me to enter our room. When it was time for dinner, he scouted around to make sure I could get in the hotel dining room. I couldn't. In order to find a place to eat, we were forced to get in the van and drive around until we found a convenient restaurant equipped for a wheelchair.

In July 1987 the *Star-Journal*, Hope, Indiana printed my article, "Being Handicapped Is Not Boring!" It was an account of our experience in Pittsburgh, Pennsylvania. There, the problem was curbs. A curb on one side was cut, but if I was to reach a cut curb on the other side of the street, it was necessary for me to take the wheelchair down a busy street. Sometimes it was quite scary.

Another incident occurred when I made a reservation at the Wisconsin Conference Center at Green Lake. We needed a campsite for our thirty-five-foot, handicap-equipped travel trailer. I talked with the housing staff months before the conference to ensure that they understood my needs. We were assured that our site was handicap accessible. As it turned out, the site was on a hill, a beautiful place immediately in front of the shower rooms. They had made sure the entrance to our trailer was as smooth as possible. It was, but on a bed of rocks. Their motive was kind, but my wheels buried in the rocks so deep that someone had to assist me up the ramp. When my husband became ill during our stay, I was trapped.

I woke up early one morning. I jumped out of bed, dressed, crawled out the back door of our trailer, and by holding onto the porch and the ramp I reached the van. I pulled myself up to the passenger's side, scooted over to the driver's seat and started the engine. I remembered a brief dialogue between the two of us while I was sneaking out the door of the trailer.

"What are you doing?" he asked in a weak voice.

"I'm taking care of myself," I answered back.

I knew I was "taking care of myself" when I turned on the ignition and heard the hum of the motor. I drove through the timberland, around BB Court. When I pulled up to the handicap parking space at the administration building, I rolled down the window and asked the first person walking by if they would please send me someone wearing a Green Lake employee tag. They did.

A lady promptly came to my rescue. I explained my problem in getting into the travel trailer. Workers extended a large board over the bed of rocks. Fortunately, my husband's condition improved. Through the remainder of the week he was able to give me a boost over the rocks approaching the board. Before leaving the conference, we selected a site for the next year to avoid such problems.

There seemed to always be a way for me to take care of myself in adverse circumstances.

2
Marriage and Parenting

The first major attack Satan made was upon the marriage God put together in the Garden of Eden. The attack started with deceit. Satan set out to prove God a liar. He's still trying to do it. He's convinced many couples that marriage doesn't mean anything anymore.

"What's a piece of paper?" Couples ask this question to avoid making or breaking wedding vows. Children involved in the situation are expected to understand why mother and daddy no longer love each other. Satan's no dummy! For the last three decades, through *consenting adults*, he has managed to break up the family structure. Couples trade one family for another as though families were merchandise. Many children have accepted the parents' self-centered attitude, which has been passed on by a society in need of healing.

Listen to the voices of parents, especially as they have reached the magic age of eighteen, when they tell you that what they do is their own *business*. In the meantime, they are digging into their bank accounts, scraping for extra income to help heal their *business*. The *consenting adult* concept has turned sour, and they have no place to turn. Whose *business* is this they have created? Marriage is tossed out the window along with love and respect for others. Loneliness, frustration, and emptiness result in their fight for independence, and we, the taxpayers, have to pick up the tab to help fix the problems.

God saw that Adam was lonely. He put him to sleep, took a rib from his side, and fashioned a woman. Then He brought her and gave her to him. Charles Swindoll says in his book, *Strike the Original Match*, to fashion is to ". . . build, to rebuild so as to cause to flourish." God fashioned that woman with marriage and family in mind.[1]

> So the Lord God caused the man to fall into a deep sleep; and while he was sleeping, he took one of the man's ribs and closed up the place with flesh. Then the Lord God made a woman from the rib he had taken out of the man, and he brought her to the man. (Gen. 2:21-22)

Adam's reaction to God's gift was that of excitement. One person paraphrased it as "WOW!"

Adam expressed gratitude for the beautiful gift God had "brought" to him. The Living Bible paraphrases Adams's reaction as, "That's it!" How many of us, when we discover the "right" person, say, "That's the one; I need not look any further?"

However we react when we are sure we've found the person with whom we wish to spend the rest of our life, we can-

---

1 Swindoll, Charles R, *Strike The Original Match*, (Minneapolis, Minnesota 55403: World Wide Publication 1980) p. 19

not overlook four "musts" that Charles Swindoll gives for a successful marriage:

1. . . . a man shall leave his father and mother (*Severance*).
2. . . . and cleave to his wife (*Permanence*).
3. . . . and they shall become one flesh (*Unity*).
4. . . . they were both naked (*Intimacy*).[2]

Why are there so many lonely people? Why are children neglected and rejected? Why have so many children of our last two generations come to the conclusion that they don't need God in their marriages? Satan is still lying to them. He has lied to them through their parents, as well as their grandparents.

"A piece of paper" is not the issue here. It's about love and respect, commitment through storms of life, and gratitude to God for the sanctity of marriage and family. It's impossible for the fourth "must" to be a reality without the others. There is no unity in sex alone. Time after time we hear the stories of loneliness and emptiness from those who have hopped in and out of bed with one person after another. They have discovered there is no complete unity without all four of these guidelines. There is no permanence in giving up one family for another.

If we live by the *consenting adults* concept, there can be no unity. Two cannot become one flesh without going through conflicts. If just *living together* is the answer, then why is there so much misery? Why have our city streets become a battlefield of misplaced children? One doesn't have to be a Christian to recognize the break down of family life. The concept

---

[2] *Ibid. p. 22*

of *consenting adults* is not the answer to happiness. The answer is more than two adults consenting to do whatever they feel like doing. It's in two people making a commitment to themselves and to God, knowing that without Him they cannot truly be one.

In 1946 I did not decide to marry Merideth without God's help. I prayed for a Christian husband before I knew he thought I was the *right* person for him. Together we looked into the future and loved our children before we said our vows in a wedding ceremony. We knew our decision to marry was not just for us. We tried to pass this concept on to our four daughters. The conflicts through which we have come in fifty years of marriage have not broken us. Rather, they have knitted us together. "No pain, no gain," it has been said.

1. We left our parents (*Severance*).
2. We stayed together through tough times (*Permanence*).
3. We became one in the flesh (*Unity*).
4. And, without these three guidelines, we could never have truly been (*Intimate*).

As I have advised many of my young married students, "If you are having marriage conflicts and you think you need to talk to someone, it is not wise to seek help from someone whose relationship is unstable. You only come away confused. However, if you talk with people who have happy relationships, you are likely to receive wise help.

❦ ❦ ❦ ❦ ❦

Ways That Seem Right Are Not Always

In the fifties our college psychologists were teaching that children should be allowed to express themselves. As a young parent and student with a toddler, I noticed that the devil was being very subtle as many young parents were gradually adopting the trend. They backed away from discipline. Several decades have gone by. Raising children with this teaching to *let them do their own thing* has contributed to the breakdown of family life. There is an overwhelming increase in divorce and crime has continued to rise.

Many of us are doing our best to care for these forgotten children, as their parents seem to have lost control. Grandparents are weeping over their children and grandchildren. Our children have listened to Satan's lies, as Eve did in the garden. "Surely you will not die," Satan insists. "It is a lie. God just knows if you eat of this tree you will know as much as he." Perhaps it is our time for which King Solomon wrote, "All a man's ways seem innocent to him" (Prov. 16:2).

Many children have difficulty knowing right from wrong. "Everything goes," they say. They have chosen their *own way.* Their *own way* has led them to sleepless nights, grieving over broken marriages and the effects on their children. They cannot be comforted, and many of them don't know why. As they search for answers from every expert available, they do not find them. Satan has them so confused that God's Word means nothing.

Nothing seems to stop the foolishness of men. Proverbs 12:15 says, "The way of the fool seems right to him, but a wise man listens to advice." Yet nobody wants to listen! God's Word is credible, and Proverbs 14:12 does not lie: "There is a way that seems right to man, but in the end it leads to death."

It *seems right* for two unmarried people to live together, or for two people of the same sex to take a child and make a family. Moreover, it *seems right* for a parent to teach a child that only Sunday morning is sufficient for their spiritual growth.

While some parents have complained because a handbook does not come with the birth of a child, it would be to their advantage to consider God's Word a perfect manual for rearing their child. Reading Proverbs 12:15, a part of God's handbook, reminds us that the way of the fool seems right to him, but a wise man listens to advice. The Holy Bible has everything we need in it to help parents. We should consult its pages and pray for understanding. If we have grandchildren who are old enough to have children, then chances are we have three generations slipping from God and us. The only thing left for us is our faith, prayer, and hope that the Spirit of God will touch them wherever they are. The same God that spoke to us through His Word, through some person or some circumstance, hasn't lost His ability to do that for our children.

I picked up the newspaper one morning. A headline jumped out at me: "Who will take care of our children?" It's a crisis, but Christian parents have hope. God has not changed since David wrote Psalm 31-32. He finished Psalm 31 with, "Love the Lord, all his saints! The Lord preserves the faithful, but the proud he pays back in full. Be strong and take heart, all you who hope in the Lord." Then he plunges into the following chapter with the blessed hope of forgiveness. He says God will instruct us in the way we should go. God will counsel us and watch over us. And that's our hope from the Lord!

I know a mother with two adult daughters. She remembers with remorse that when they were small she failed to give them all her attention and show them what Jesus is like. Both of the daughters have since chosen a lifestyle that has brought them dishonor. This mother cannot bring back the past and correct her neglect for them. However, since the time they were teenagers, she has prayed daily for God to show them. She has repented of what she has contributed to their life, and she knows God has forgiven her. She has discussed with them how she has failed them. They have forgiven her. She has forgiven them. Very slowly they are searching and finding their own way with the Lord. That mother still claims God's promises for her daughters as she continues to pray for them. It is a family matter now. The daughters, one married with four small children, and the grandparents have joined together in the name of Jesus for healing. God is honoring the parents' prayers, and a complete healing is certain with this family. They know that what seemed to them to be right a few years ago is sinfully wrong, and they are healing.

It is possible that we as parents and grandparents have listened to too many voices. What the voices say may seem right, but often they are not.

$$\text{\emph{\&}\quad\text{\emph{\&}}\quad\text{\emph{\&}}\quad\text{\emph{\&}}\quad\text{\emph{\&}}}$$

Excuses

Sometimes our children come up with excuses for not going to church. Do we negotiate with them? If they suddenly decide that school is boring and they do not need to go, do we negotiate? Most of us are firm about the importance of school. How about the importance of spiritual growth? My husband and I tried to exercise the same parental authority in spiritual matters as we did in education. Our four daughters were not thrilled to go to school at times. In spite of that, they learned enough to graduate from high school, and one of them made it through college. Sometimes, going to church wasn't their *cup of tea*, but they were exposed to the truth of God. As they learned some values from going to school, they learned some values from going to church school and worship.

"My parents forced me to go to school. That is why I disrespect education, teachers and educators." We rarely hear such statements, but people will say, "My parents forced me to go to church. That is why I disrespect Christianity and the church." How do we react to these excuses?

Satan, the father of lies, is sneaky. He puts it in the minds of our children to give excuses about boring church and dry sermons. He never stops.

We are most vulnerable to Satan's cunning lies when we are not grounded in the Word of God. He knows that parents won't listen to excuses about whether their children should be educated, so he tells us we are turning our children away from church by making them go. And he cons our teenagers into the idea of skipping youth meetings or church.

Our granddaughter once came to us, saying, "I'm not getting anything out of church, it's boring. Besides, nearly all the kids are leaving after the youth meeting." She wasn't appealing to us to be absent from the youth meeting at that point. She was manipulating. She wanted to leave after the youth meeting and miss worship. Having much experience with such teenage manipulation, I asked her what she planned to do during the worship hour.

"Nearly all the kids are leaving," she said, adding, "and we're not doing anything wrong. The kids have been going to Tim's house just to hang out for a while, just having fun."

Tim was a deacon's son, and I knew his parents would be at church. They were probably unaware that he had been having kids over while they were at church.

I didn't lecture her. "I'm sure you would enjoy the party, Deanette, but most people I know who become disinterested in church only intended to miss just this one time."

My definite, but gentle answer was no. She settled back on the couch, pouted a little, and we all went to church. Guess what? Most all of her friends were in church. Her mood brightened by the time the service was over. It is so important that we do not send conflicting messages to our children. We can let them know what our priorities are without preaching to them.

Think about it. Chances are that when these excuses come from your teenagers, they will have something already planned during that hour you spend in church.

A grieving mother later told me that as soon as she started giving in to the excuses of her teenage daughter, the girl began slipping away from church. It was so gradual that she didn't notice at first. Some of her daughter's friends followed. Once they slipped away, they were difficult to reach. That mother felt responsible for all the young people who had left. Her daughter was one of those who began skipping church to go where Deanette had requested to go.

Jesus once said to some disciples, "Will ye also go away?" Remember, one never slips away alone.

🌿 🌿 🌿 🌿 🌿

Let Go and Let God

We adopted three of our four daughters. In 1960 we doubled our family.

Our biological daughter, Gwen, was eleven when we received a call from the Child Welfare Department of Arkansas. When the director called to say she had found a little sister for Gwen, she tossed in a challenge. Annette, who was nine, had a sister, eleven. We agreed to meet them before making our final decision to take both of them.

It was an exciting day on April 15, 1960. With her teacher's permission, we took Gwen out of school. It was imperative that she come with us, for she would share in our decision to accept both children. The Child Welfare director greeted us, motioned for us to have a seat while she briefed us on the children. Then she left the three of us alone to think about it. We were anxious as we waited for her to return with them. After spending some time with these two little girls, we opened our arms and hearts to them. Our answer was yes, and they agreed to go home with us.

Later, we learned that in an office a few doors away from our meeting place were two small children. The girls' brother, six, and their little sister, four, were meeting their prospective parents. Although they had been with case workers and foster parents for three years preparing them for this moment, it saddened us to learn that the four children were separated. We were not allowed to meet them, but Annette and Katy were given some time to have a last visit before they said farewell to their little sister and brother, possibly never to see them again.

Bringing two little girls into the parsonage at Bald Knob, Arkansas was exciting. However, it was the beginning of domestic and emotional adjustments. Annette, the nine-year-old, was slow to accept us as her family. Katy and Gwen, each eleven, shared a bedroom. Annette had her private room and missed Katy, who had been a little mother to her. She also grieved over the loss of her younger siblings. Seeing the problem, we moved her into the room with Gwen and Katy. That arrangement helped some, but it was not until Mary, nine, joined our family that we noticed a remarkable improvement. They were playmates. They bonded quickly, and Annette was beginning to accept us. Mary, who was only three weeks younger than Annette, was God's answer to our problem.

Before we knew it, our four daughters were grown up. Each entered a life of her own. We watched them through their teen years as they made right and wrong decisions. Sometimes their choices caused us anxiety, but Merideth and I knew we never lost when we let go. We gained their love and friendship. As someone has stated, "To love is to let go." We agreed to never try to pressure them in their adult decisions, and as far as I know we were true to that agreement.

The idea of bringing hurt children into our home for a *quick fix* failed. There was no sudden change, but upon the authority God had given us as parents, we felt secure in His love and grace for the task. With consistent faith in His Word, we prayed for each one of them to be successful in life. We coped with disappointments when two of them went astray, but communication between us has been open throughout their adult years.

There comes a time when we must let go and *let God have His way* with our children. Of course, they'll make mistakes. So did we. We could do no less than pattern our parenting after our Heavenly Father. We guide them when they are small and nourish them when they are hungry. The Father's way with His children is to help us grow up in Him. At some point He lets us go to make decisions about Him and our relationship with Him. We make bad choices, and we suffer the consequences, but we are not alone. He accepts our confession and forgives us. He lets go until we have learned our lessons well. We must let go until our children have learned their lessons well.

Evangelizing Our Children

Gwen accepted Christ when she was five. Our responsibility increased. Would we be able to guide our new daughters from three different environments to Christ?

First, we had to get acquainted with them. It was not easy for them to run freely to us with their problems. Calling us mother and daddy took some getting used to. No problem arose with two of them.

But with Mary, the youngest, it was different. Prior to her adoption, she had lived with us and called us Mr. and Mrs. Wilfong long enough that saying "mother" was very difficult for her. We gave her time, however, and the day she called me "mother" was a time to remember. Once she had said it, she no longer had problems calling us "mother" and "daddy."

The children's profession of faith in Jesus Christ came sooner than we had anticipated. Katy, the eldest and an avid reader, came to know Christ through reading the Bible. I'll never forget her announcement as she came charging into the kitchen. I could barely hear her voice above the clattering dishes.

"Mother," she said. "I was reading the Bible and found out how I could become God's child. It said if I called upon the name of the Lord, I would be saved."

"Well, what happened?" I asked.

"I did what He said. I got down on my knees by my bed and asked him to save me. He did." She spoke with confidence, adding, "I believe Jesus died for me. I believe He was buried and that He arose, and now He is with God in heaven." I embraced her and shared her joy.

Katy's conversion encouraged us. Soon after her decision, her biological sister, Annette, who was ten at the time, responded to an invitation at church. Merideth had the joy of baptizing Annette and Katy.

"One more to go," I thought. Our ten-year-old, Mary, so small she wore a size eight dress, seemed unimpressed with Katy's and Annette's new life in Christ. This spicy little blue-eyed, blond girl bounced right into the midst of our family, but was taking her time about accepting Christ. I watched her wait out one invitation after another. She appeared to be under conviction, but for some reason was fighting it. Mary was a spunky little girl, self sufficient and independent. No matter how she was reprimanded or punished, she never cried a tear. She seemed immune to pain and resisted conviction like a seasoned adult.

Early one morning I was sitting in my favorite chair reading the Bible. I heard some definite, quick footsteps behind me. Only Mary walked like that. She reached my side, leaned against me, waiting for me to respond.

"Good morning," I said, embracing her and drawing her gently onto my lap.

"Good morning," she responded in her squeaky little voice, so perfect with her warm and spicy personality. Then she added, "wha'cha doin'?"

"Oh, I'm reading from God's Word. Do you want to join me?" I asked.

With my Bible where Nicodemus had come to Jesus in the night (John 3), I invited her to read aloud to me. She read Jesus' answer to Nicodemus' question about how to be saved.

"Mary, do you ever think about giving your life to Jesus?" I asked.

"Yes," she responded, her head lowered, still in a reading position. It was obvious she was avoiding the discussion. However, she raised her head and began to talk to me freely.

She told me why she hadn't gone forward during the invitations at church. Her explanation also uncovered the mystery of why she never cried. When she was very young, the adults in her family called her a "baby" if she cried. She had an uncle who had abused her verbally and physically, adding more pain and fear to her life. She was taught to be tough. Crying was not appropriate anywhere, any time.

"I want to go up," she said. "But I notice whenever people get saved and go up to daddy at the altar, they cry. I'm afraid I'll cry."

"It's OK to cry," I assured her and pointed at the scripture where Jesus wept.

It wasn't easy, but I was successful in helping her understand that crying was not a sign of weakness, but a sign of feeling.

"People cry because they are sorry for their sins, and they cry because they are happy when they learn how much God loves them. When they trust their lives to Jesus, they become a child of God and they cry tears of joy." I tried to help her understand. Then I said, "Do you remember when we received the final papers saying you were our daughter, and your name would be Mary Wilfong?"

"Yes," she replied as her eyes lit up.

"And do you remember how we wept and hugged each other? That was because we felt so happy," I explained.

Shortly after that incident, Annette expressed to Mary how she had accepted Christ. Mary responded to her sister by saying yes to Jesus as they knelt beside the bed. She followed through with a public profession of her faith and was baptized.

What a wonderful privilege it is for family members to help each other to know Christ. Each child is different and responds in individual ways, but baptism is their expression of faith in Christ, His death, burial, and resurrection.

❧ ❧ ❧ ❧ ❧

Father Leads Son to Jesus

My brother once wrote his story of how my father had led him to Jesus: "In our little community there was only one church building. It belonged to the Methodist congregation, who shared their house of worship with the Baptist congregation.

"The Baptist pastor preached one weekend, and the Methodist pastor preached the next. Therefore, there was a joint service each Sunday.

"Each year the two congregations cooperated in a joint revival meeting. It was at one of those annual meetings, September 1941, that I became convicted of my need for Jesus. The Holy Spirit tugged at my heart, waking me up during the night. However, I was a very shy eleven-year-old who avoided crowds. It wasn't so much that I was afraid of what people would say. I was just afraid. Each evening my fears discouraged me from walking down the aisle to make a public confession.

"For me, each night of that week had been sleepless, but Thursday night was worse than the others. Friday morning I awakened with a heavy heart. After breakfast I could resist the Holy Spirit no longer. I must tell mother. My two sisters were helping mother clean up after breakfast. I finally got up enough nerve to share my feelings. Mother said nothing. She simply stopped what she was doing, walked to the back door, and called Dad in from the stock lot where he was doing some morning chores. He sat his milk bucket down on the table and took me by the hand.

"'Come on, son, let's you and I go to the barn,' he said.

"I had been taken to the barn before during my eleven years, but for different reasons. This time there was a spirit of love and compassion flowing from my father that I had felt few times before. In silence we walked to the barn, my hand grasped very gently in his. We sat on one of the foundation logs of the barn just outside the corn crib. He began to ask me some very direct questions about the morals of my life. My confession began. During the summer we had stayed overnight at my Aunt Lula's house. It wasn't unusual for cousins and siblings to sleep together in those days. Because of a shortage of sleeping arrangements, I was forced to sleep in the same bed with my youngest sister and my cousin. My sister thought that my cousin and I were getting too friendly and told my parents about it. Therefore, the questions I was asked were directed toward that event.

"When my father was satisfied with the answers I had given, he directed his questions to my relationship with the Lord; questions like, 'do you know what sin is?' And, 'If you should die today, do you know where you would spend eternity?' I gave him the answers with a nod of the head, but my eyes were fixed on the ground in front of me. When he was convinced that I understood what I must do, he took me by the hand. We stepped into the corn crib. Once inside, we dropped to our knees, and he began to pray for my salvation. At the same time, I began to pray silently. I acknowledged Jesus as Lord and asked Him to come into my life. At that very moment the burden of sin rolled off my shoulders, and a peace that I had never known before flooded my soul. I looked into the eyes of my father. I could see that he knew what had happened to me. We embraced each other while still on our knees, crying tears of joy. It is the first time I ever saw my father cry. It was great!

"That evening we arrived at the church grounds earlier than usual. The first person I saw was my best friend. As always, we began running and playing among the trees. Before we went into the church building for the service, it was among the trees that I told my friend what had happened to me that morning. His response was little more than a nod of his head, and we went on with our playing.

"My mind was made up. I knew I would respond to the invitation after the service. The joy in my heart far exceeded the fear of appearing before people. I sang the songs with more feeling and gave more attention to the sermon than ever before. Before the first stanza was finished, I was in the aisle and on my way to make public my profession of faith.

"The evangelist prayed with me, and I turned to find my place on the front pew. To my surprise, I glanced out of the corner of my eye and saw my friend talking with the Methodist evangelist. I didn't talk to my friend about it. I prefer to think that his decision was influenced by the witness I had given under the trees before the service. The following Sunday afternoon, at the close of the revival meeting, twenty-six were baptized.

"My life has never been the same. A new and wonderful awareness of the presence of God's Holy Spirit filled my very being."[3]

I remember my brother's conversion as though it happened yesterday. The image is clear. I could see that Daddy had the ultimate answer to Leslie's questions tucked under his left arm, the Bible. He lovingly caressed Leslie's hand as they entered the barn. While this young lad was making the most important decision in his life, a discussion was in progress back in the kitchen. My mother, my sister, and I suspected that something good was happening at the barn. In the meantime, we prayed.

---

3 Leslie N. Chadwick, Th.D, Author of *The Unity of the Body of Christ*, 1996

After her prayer, mother said, "Something will happen before they return, you'll see."

She was right. It was no surprise to see the happy expressions on their faces when they came out of the barn. The ray of glowing victory and the spring in Daddy and Leslie's steps confirmed mother's prediction. This childhood confession was the beginning of a life in Christ that led my brother into the pastoral ministry. What if Daddy had not been there for him? What if he had been one of our latchkey kids today, who might attend a revival meeting? Who would be there for them to answer their questions as they searched for salvation?

A verbal announcement of a child's new birth in Christ was not necessary to inform those of us who were waiting in the kitchen. We knew that God had blessed the relationship between father and son. However, it was necessary for Leslie to share his experience. I know the angels were rejoicing, as the hugging and crying for joy continued for a few moments. A heavy burden had been lifted from the shoulders of a small boy. It was always a family celebration when one of us accepted Christ.

Although he is disabled and had to discontinue the pastoral ministry, Leslie continues to evangelize through his writing and personal evangelism. The love and compassion which I've seen in him since he was a young boy is shown in his relationship with others. Such love comes from the Son of God, and no other love can exceed the love of a "Holy God," as Leslie puts it.

Therefore since we have been justified through faith, we have peace with God through our Lord Jesus Christ, through whom we have gained access by faith into this grace in which we now stand. And we rejoice in the hope of the glory of God. Not only so, but we also rejoice in our sufferings, because we know that suffering produces perseverance, character, and hope. And hope does not disappoint us, because God has poured out his love into our hearts by the Holy Spirit, whom he has given us. (Rom. 5:1-5)

One never knows what God's plan for a child's life is. As parents, are we prepared to help our children through this decision making process. Shouldn't we evangelize our own children?

3
Children

Years of working with young parents taught me much about God's little ones. When parents brought their little children to Jesus, the disciples rebuked them. Unpleased with their indignation, He said to them, "Let the little children come to me, and do not hinder them, for the kingdom of God belongs to such as these" (Mark 10:14). He took the children in his arms, put his hands on them, and blessed them.

The eagerness of parents to have Jesus touch their little ones was best demonstrated by a group of young parents I once taught in church school. As the Young Adult Department grew, so did the nursery and children's departments grow. Once a month the Good News Class had a pitch-in lunch in the Fellowship Hall. Each time the children filtered in I witnessed a re-enactment of the passage in Mark. There was one exception, however. The disciples in our church welcomed each child. A special place was provided for each age group as their department grew, and those little ones became part of the larger family, the Church.

One Sunday I noticed how the children enjoyed each other. Two small girls stretched their little arms to their full length to grasp the handles of a couple of baby strollers. The babies were happy passengers who were as delighted as their caretakers were. Other children were running to the kitchen, where their mothers were preparing the food. Responsible fathers kept a watchful eye on their children, while they chatted among themselves. It was a pleasant family spirit! Christian love was expressed in cheerful voices from every corner of the hall. These parents were "permitting," or "letting," their little ones come unto Jesus.

As Christ taught his early disciples, He teaches us. If we are to enter the kingdom of God, we must be like little children. Our Sundays together brought a fresh meaning to the words of Christ, to be as little children. How can our little ones experience the Master's blessed touch if we do not bring them to meet him?

⚜ ⚜ ⚜ ⚜ ⚜

CHRISTMAS REFLECTION (NO TOYS UNDER OUR TREE)

I remember when I was seven. Christmas was drawing near. Times were hard, and my father was struggling to put food on the table. He explained to us that we shouldn't get our hopes up for Santa's visit. There just wasn't enough money for Christmas that year, but Daddy always made sure that we had a tree. Mother would help us string popcorn with which to garnish it. There were very few ornaments, all of which were handmade. Decorating the tree was the most fun. We didn't notice that we had placed most of the trimmings and ornaments on the front branches.

It was sometimes difficult for us to tell when Daddy, being the tease he was, was joking. Since it was not the first time for him to warn us that we should not get our hopes up, we chose to think he was just teasing. He always managed to come up with presents under the tree.

It was traditional on Christmas Eve for our parents to tuck us in for the night, saying, "Now you hurry and go to sleep. Santa won't come as long as you are awake." However, this particular Christmas seemed a little different. It was as though we could sense an atmosphere of sadness when they tucked us in that Christmas Eve. They didn't give us the normal instructions. But then, we thought, they probably just forgot, or Daddy was supporting his tease. They would come through. They always did. So my sister and I ignored the advice that we were not to get excited. I closed my eyelids tight and pretended not to worry. I listened for a sound from my sister. When it was obvious she wasn't sleeping either, I nudged her for a response.

"Gerry, are you asleep?" I whispered.

"No, but be quiet" she cautioned.

I just had to ask: "Do you think Daddy and Mother really have no presents for us?"

"I think we'll get something. I think they are teasing," she said, and we giggled quietly. We agreed that Daddy was just kidding. He just thought he had us fooled!

Visions of toys for the little brothers and a big doll for Gerry and me under the tree filled my head. Would my doll be able to stand or walk, or would she be a baby doll that sucked her bottle and wet her diaper? My visions and questions filtered from my mind as I dozed off.

On Christmas morning we jumped out of bed as we always had, and quietly rushed to the living room. I was frozen in my steps at the sight of the tree. There were no toys, not a single gift under the tree. There was no doll for the girls, no toys for the boys. I thought my chest would burst with disappointment. To keep from crying, I caught my breath, looked around to see if I had overlooked something.

"Daddy's really taking this thing too far," I thought. I turned to Gerry. "He's really teasing us this time," I said. "Do you think he might have our presents hidden some place? He'll come up with them later don't you think?"

I was hopeful. I remembered one Christmas he waited until the last minute and suddenly appeared with large shopping bags full of gifts. We waited, expecting Daddy to charge through one of those doors with something. He came in the room, but there was nothing in his hands, and he looked sad.

Noon came. Still, no surprise. The expression on each face told us it was time to give up. We were finally convinced that there really would be no gifts. My disappointment turned to sympathy, sympathy for my parents. As small as I was, I wanted to hug each of them and tell them it was OK. I snuggled up to my father and told him not to worry.

As usual, my parents talked about whose birthday it was and that Christ was the main gift. We knew that, but somehow it didn't take care of my feelings. It was still not Christmas without presents. I don't remember what we had for dinner that Christmas Day, and I had put the possibility of a surprise gift to rest. I remember standing on our front porch watching the neighbor's little girl enjoy her new bike. In my childish envy, I drooled with a vision of having my own bike.

Daddy left for a while that afternoon. He returned with a smile on his face and holding a paper bag with something in it. His explanation was that he had met Santa Claus downtown. Santa Claus had been unable to get into our house.

Reaching into the bag, Daddy said, "So here is what he left." Then he drew out two little, rubber, squeaky dolls. "One for you, Rachel, and one for Gerry."

As he handed them to us I thought, *"What kind of Santa would only have 'leftovers' for any child?"*

Nevertheless, we accepted them, somehow thinking good things about our Daddy who had done his best. He explained that, unable to endure our disappointment, he had gone to a friend's house. A man who owned the drug store in our little town was moved by my father's story. He opened up his store to let Daddy pick out a gift for each child. He could pay later.

Never a Christmas goes by that I do not reflect upon that day. Drug stores today have a variety of items, unlike Mr. Chapel's store, where the toys came from. When I see the world of toys available and money with which to buy them, I thank God for reminding me of that Christmas when there was nothing under the tree. More vivid than my personal disappointment, was the hurt I saw on my parents' faces. They couldn't even buy a little gift for each of their four children. Now, I remember that they did the best they could.

> And the King shall answer and say unto them, verily I say unto you, inasmuch as ye have done it unto one of the least of these my brethren, ye have done it unto me. (Matt. 25:40 KJV)

ɬ ɬ ɬ ɬ ɬ

GOD'S LIKE MY DADDY

There was a five-year-old who was obviously thrilled with God's mighty adventures in the Good Book. For his bedtime prayer, the lad said, "I sure like your science fiction stories in the Bible, God, can you tell me where you get them?"

Sometimes it is quite a challenge for adults to help children understand the difference between science fiction and reality. Several years ago I directed children's church. My storyteller was our associate minister's wife. With her genuine cheerful spirit, along with attractive visual aids, Gloria made Bible characters come alive. Together we planned for each Sunday. Father's Day was coming up. How could we explain to a room full of little ones what God is like? We prayerfully tried.

It was Father's Day. Chairs were placed in a semicircle, and the music to call them to worship began. When it stopped, each child took the nearest chair. An atmosphere for worship was automatically created with their cheerful voices singing songs of worship and praise. This order of activity prepared them for story time.

Immediately, Gloria captured their attention. "What do you think God looks like?"

A four-year-old lad knew exactly what God looked like. With wide, expressive blue eyes looking directly into Gloria's, he planted both feet on the floor, positioned his energetic little body as if to be on an Olympic starting line, and spoke. "God looks like . . . He . . . He-e-e looks . . . just like my Daddy . . . ." Then stretching to his full height, reaching both hands high above his head, he blurted out, "Only a lot bigger!"

A storyteller's work is made easier if a child pictures God looking and acting like his or her Christian father. If the emulation that God is "like my Daddy" is true, fathers would be wise to consider, "Would it be OK if my child sees God as he sees me?"

A five-year-old came up with this explanation for why there is but one God: "Because God fills every place and there's no room for another one."

♧ ♧ ♧ ♧ ♧

THELMA

As I have mentioned earlier, our family experienced a growth explosion during the summer of 1960. Remember Mary? When she joined the family, she solved a problem with Annette. At first Mary came to live with us temporarily, but by Christmas that year she was legally adopted.

Mary's family migrated from Florida to Bald Knob, Arkansas during strawberry picking season. Because of family illness, the ministers of the town cooperated in finding a place to rent for them. After winter, they could return to their home in Florida. The Welfare Assistance Agent approached us concerning Mary. He asked if we would let her live with us so she could stay in school. The second child of four, she was self sufficient at the age of nine. Her expenses would be covered by the department. Still adjusting to two extra daughters, being a mother of another wasn't so bad. Winter was approaching quickly. School was in full swing, and each girl must pass a mother's inspection before walking out that front door to school.

A checklist went like this: "Got on your warm underwear? Are your socks straight? Oh yes, did you get your ears clean? And don't forget to brush your teeth."

This story, however, is really about Thelma, Mary's eleven-year-old sister. Like Mary, Thelma was very small for her age, undernourished, and neglected. Thelma and two small siblings were still living with their parents. They were not aware that they would soon be in the custody of the Child Welfare Department.

Winter weather was a little ahead of schedule that fall. Wind howled around our door in late September. After giving our four daughters their last-minute inspection before going to school, they would step out from the cozy three-bedroom parsonage into the brisk air.

Just as I was helping the girls with their coats, a light knock came at the front door. Who could be calling this early on a very, cool morning? I went to the door. Before the warm moisture could cover the storm door to cloud my vision, I recognized Thelma.

Frail, sickly little Thelma was hunched over in her tattered clothes. Her feet were exposed to the cold weather, and on her chapped, blue hands were no gloves. She looked like a little old lady bent under a cold, heavy load. Merideth and I were involved in Thelma's treatment at the University of Arkansas in Little Rock. She had serious and complex medical problems. Although she had been released from the hospital a couple of days earlier, her treatments would continue indefinitely. Unlike Mary, who was self-sufficient and still in school, Thelma was a special child and needed special, tender loving care and constant supervision. Needless to say, I was surprised to see her.

"M-zz We'fon', can I come in with Mur-r-ry?" she spoke through her thin, blue lips.

"Of course, Thelma," I said, adding, "What are you doing out so early on this cold morning?"

Clasping her bony, frozen hands in mine, I helped Thelma inside. Her little fingers seemed to snap under the pressure of mine. "Here, honey, come over here and stand over the furnace vent where it's warm," I said.

Shivering, Thelma bent over the floor vent. I wiped her runny nose with a tissue and held her close to me to speed up the warming process. With tears in her eyes, and strands of stringy, brown hair hanging over her face, she whined, "M-zz We'fon', I wanna live here with Mur-r-ry."

My heart turned to mush. How could I explain to Thelma why she could not stay with Mary. She couldn't possibly understand why a strange lady with the welfare department must take care of her. I turned to the other girls who were concerned about Thelma and told them to go on to school, that I would take care of Thelma. They slowly went out the door.

After I gave Thelma some warm food, I took her back to her parents. She could not understand why she wasn't included with our family. That little girl's face haunts me yet. Frustrated? Yes, and fighting tears, I wanted to say, "Yes, you can stay here with Mary."

As it turned out, the three remaining children were placed in foster homes. A few months later the caseworker brought Thelma by. Her treatments had done wonders for her skin and her underdevelopment. She appeared to be happy. The parents returned to Florida, and Mary became our legally adopted daughter.

🍃 🍃 🍃 🍃 🍃

THE LITTLE MISSIONARY

Janet's eyes sparkled with excitement. She had just arrived with her parents at their new home in a country called Indonesia. This little eight-year-old with dark hair and brown eyes was the daughter of missionaries.

Janet liked being a child of a missionary couple, because missionaries made many friends. She had often pretended she was a missionary like her parents. But she thought, "How can a little girl be a real missionary — especially a girl who has a handicap?" You see, Janet could not walk and talk as well as most children.

Janet moved all through the house and around the yard as quickly as she could. Her new home was different from those in the United States, and her curiosity sent her touching the leaves on the plants and smelling the flowers. Some dirt slipped through her fingers as she answered her mother's call.

"Want to go with me to the market, Janet?" mother asked.

"Oh yes!" Janet replied as she waddled up to her mother and took her hand. "Will there be some little girls there?"

"I'm sure there will be children, Janet," and, holding hands, mother and daughter went off to the market.

Janet's heart was beating fast with excitement. She tried to hurry, but her legs and feet didn't obey her mind very well. She stumbled frequently as she became more anxious.

"Slow down!" Her mother cautioned. "You're going to fall and take me with you."

"It's a market outdoors, mother. Look!" Janet interrupted and awkwardly pointed toward the marketplace.

"Yes, it is. Do you see any children?" They both looked over the crowd of people around the market tables.

"Children! Look mommy, some children!" Janet's keen eyes had spotted a group of boys and girls huddled together. Mother held her hand tightly to keep her from breaking away.

But Janet drew back when she noticed the children laughing and pointing at her. Her hand clutched her mother's tightly. She felt disappointed as she moved closer to her mother for protection.

"Mother, why are the children laughing at me?" Janet could hardly keep back the tears.

"Well, Janet, it's probably because they don't know you yet, and you look different to them." Her mother spoke softly when she noticed how sad Janet was. "But I'll bet when they get to know you they won't laugh at you."

"Janet went home dejected. It wasn't at all like she had expected. At bedtime her mother took her on her lap and tried to make her feel better.

"Don't cry," she whispered, "It will be all right. We'll ask Jesus to help them understand you."

Janet felt safe in her mother's comforting arms. Soon she fell asleep.

The next time they went to the marketplace Janet saw the same children. They were snickering as they had done before.

Leaving her mother's side, Janet moved a little closer to them. She swallowed hard, then bravely said, "Please don't laugh at me; I won't laugh at you." But they didn't understand her.

She stepped back near her mother and asked, "Mother, do you suppose if I sing for them they will stop laughing at me?"

"Yes, Janet, why don't you sing for them – that might just work." She agreed.

Janet began to sing. As she sang about Jesus, one by one the children gathered around her. They liked to hear her sing. She never stopped singing while her mother did her shopping. And she sang all the way back to her house.

To Janet's amazement, the children followed them to her yard. She turned around, smiled, and waved. Her mother suggested that she invite them to visit a while.

"Oh, may I? They like me now, don't they?" And with a spring in her step she went toward them and motioned for them to come into her yard.

The children played for a long time. Since Janet's mother knew their language, they understood her when she asked them if their parents might be looking for them. She suggested they go home and come back the next day. They waved goodbye, chattering as they left. Janet was certain that they would be back to play with her. And she was right. The very next day her new friends returned.

That's when Janet's mother came up with an idea. "Janet, would you like to be a real missionary? You can tell your new friends about Jesus and how much He loves them."

"I can?" Janet asked. "Can I really be a missionary?"

"Of course, you can," She responded.

Janet watched her mother as she built shelves from some wooden boxes. On one shelf, she placed storybooks and Christian comics. On the bottom shelf, she placed toys. Both the books and toys could be reached easily by the smallest children. Each day Janet could hardly wait until they arrived. They learned how to talk with her and her mother. With the help of the books and the Bible, they learned how much Jesus loved them.

As the days and weeks went by the children were able to read that Jesus is God's only Son, and that He died for their sins. With her mother, Janet was able to help some of them ask Jesus into their hearts.

Sometimes Janet's friends would ask questions that were too hard for her. She would take them by the hand and say, "Come, we'll ask Mother."

Before long, the children were speaking English very well. When they saw Janet and her mother at the market, or driving down the street, they shouted big and loud in English, "Hi, Janet's mother – Hi, Janet!" No longer was Janet sad. No longer did the children laugh at the way she walked and talked. She was so happy to have them like her. But most of all she was happy she had told them about her best friend, Jesus.

One night when Janet's mother tucked her in, she said, "Mother, am I a real missionary yet?"

"You bet," said her mother. "Sweet dreams my little missionary."[1]

---

[1] "The Little Missionary" by Rachel Wilfong appeared in the November/December 1991 issue of *Evangelizing Today's Child* (Warrenton, MO 63383) p. 63

🌿 🌿 🌿 🌿 🌿

A Tiny Funnel of Flour

My husband and I went on a preaching mission trip to Central America. The package of information we received prior to our trip included the health risks we would be taking. Hazardous conditions of contaminated food and water were explained carefully, and it would be up to us to follow the instructions once we were there. The hostesses, where twenty-one North Americans would be staying, had attended a workshop to help them prepare food for us, with an emphasis on sanitation.

Our first week was in Tippitapa, Nicaragua. Pastor Carlos Rojas and his wife, Gracia, were prepared to be our hosts. They lived in an extension of the church with their four children and Gracia's brother, Benjamin. The church was an old, but well built structure, with genuine tile-covered floors. Our tiny bedroom was a Sunday School room behind the sanctuary with small, single cots for our beds. In order to get to the room, we went through the sanctuary into a rather long room. We were awakened early each morning by a squeaking mop put in motion by a fourteen-year-old girl. Maria was hired by our Mission Board to help Gracia. She kept the genuine tile mirror clean.

The tiny rooms where the family lived were hardly adequate for this family of seven. The parents slept in the room directly behind the church. Four children slept in the center room, and meals were prepared in a dark, crowded kitchen. Gracia prepared her food in a square, dingy, cement sink, with no running water. She cooked on a two-burner stove and washed the dishes in the inadequate sink. Our meals were served on a long table in the Sunday School room next to our room.

When we filled out our papers for the trip, we requested to stay in a home with children. Our request was granted, but we were disappointed that their culture did not allow us to eat with the mother and children. After Gracia served her guests and husband, she returned to the kitchen. She ate with her children at a round table surrounded by boxes, a small icebox, and scarcely enough room for the chairs in which they sat.

"Why can't we eat with Gracia and the children?" I boldly asked my interpreter.

She turned to Carlos and in Spanish interpreted my question. His direct response was to face Merideth, speaking in Spanish. Translated into English, his remark was, "When you are in North America, you boss; in Nicaragua, I boss." Everyone chuckled.

A few days passed before Gracia allowed me in her kitchen. That was the day that Benjamin, her teenage brother, shimmied up a coconut tree to get me a coconut. He slid back down to the ground and handed the coconut to Doris, our interpreter. I followed her to the kitchen and waited at the open door. Gracia motioned for me to enter with Doris. I was interested in seeing Doris open the coconut and extract the juice, but more interested in permission to see inside the living quarters of this humble family. After she showed me their rooms, Gracia overcame her shyness. Henceforth, we became good friends.

Gracia was surprised when I asked her if I could cook an American breakfast some morning. Once she understood my request, she reluctantly consented and asked me what I needed to prepare the breakfast. My American breakfast consisted of fried potatoes, scrambled eggs, and gravy. She had everything but flour for the gravy, so she sent her five-year-old daughter to the open marketplace to buy some. The little girl returned shortly. With her round, smiling face, her huge brown eyes fixed on me, she lifted up a small paper funnel filled with flour.

Little did I know the cost of that tiny bit of flour. Neither was I aware that it was an exception rather than a rule for Gracia to have flour in her kitchen. I was not aware that she had emptied her flour supply. Nor did I know that the tiny portion of flour in the homemade paper funnel had cost enough money to buy a full day's supply of food for the family? However, the expression on her little daughter's brown face revealed sheer joy and a satisfaction that I was pleased. I tried to hide the mixed emotions I was feeling for the little girl's joy and sadness for the poverty around me. In my heart I asked God to forgive me for the imposition I had caused.

I prepared the American breakfast while Gracia looked on. I had so much to learn. Those little children were not impressed with my fixings. It had not occurred to me that, like our children in America, they were unimpressed with foreign food; they knew what potatoes and eggs were, but gravy? What was that pasty looking stuff?

As I reflect upon the funnel of flour and the food so graciously prepared by a loving host, I do not think of the dingy, crowded kitchen where it was cooked. I think of the love that went into weeks of planning from the heart of a couple who hardly had enough food to nourish their family.

A missionary from Haiti was once a guest in our home. I learned that the reason he ate so little was because he was thinking of his people who were starving. He felt that he had no right to eat while they had nothing. I don't think I can help my poor friends by refusing to eat what I have before me, but I do know that God wants me to remember this experience and see that it is multiplied all over the world. My mission giving must be consistent for those who depend upon mission dollars for their survival.

Paul talks about loving money and what we buy with it. "But godliness with contentment is great gain. For we brought nothing into the world, and we can take nothing out of it. But if we only have food and clothing, we will be content with that" (I Tim. 6:6-8).

4
Pain and Suffering

Did you ever question God about His mysterious ways? Jeremiah did. "You are always righteous, O Lord, when I bring a case before you. Yet I would speak with you about your justice: Why does the way of the wicked prosper? Why do all the faithless live at ease?" He complained in Jeremiah 12:1. Why do the ungodly have so much and righteous have so little?

Other mysteries puzzle us. How about the mystery of the union of Christ with the church? Paul says in Ephesians 5:32, "This is a profound mystery — but I am talking about Christ and the church." He talks about the union of husband and wife.

Does the mystery of suffering ever disturb you? "No discipline seems pleasant at the time, but painful. Later on, however, it produces a harvest of righteousness and peace for those who have been trained by it" (Heb. 12:11).

My automatic reaction to God, when my plans are interrupted, is to ask, "OK, Lord, what are you trying to tell me now?" Experiences in my disability have taught me about God's ways in my life. I know that He loves me, and that He will not allow anything to happen to me which is not good for me. "And we know that in all things God works for the good of those who love him, who have been called according to his purpose" (Rom. 8:28).

Answers to my questions may not come for days, but I rest my case on His mysterious ways. I know that whatever His plan is for me, it has to be better than anything I could imagine. The longer it takes for me to learn what He's up to, the better the revelation is. There is some kind of sweetness in waiting upon the Lord, as I experience His faithfulness and grace.

"I have much more to say to you, more than you can now bear" (John 16:12). In my human weakness I reach out to Him with palms up to receive what I need. I trust my weaknesses and my strengths to Him, and I find myself leaning on Him. His loving arms are waiting no matter how long it takes for me to recognize the intended blessing.

The Bible is contemporary. Our search for more effective ways to serve the Lord is best satisfied as we consume His Words. Without God, our search for answers in education, attending workshops, etc., can only bring confusion. Perhaps for a while they seem to help, but it is the Word of God that fits every problem in every situation.

His instructions in Matthew 21:21 worked for me when our four daughters were growing up. Speaking to a mountain in life still works today. After all the wise counsel in books and all the suggestions from newspaper columnists, we hear God's words still saying, "Do not conform any longer to the pattern of this world, but be transformed by the renewing of your mind. Then you will be able to test and approve what

God's will is—his good, pleasing and perfect will" (Rom. 12:2).

"Therefore, we do not lose heart. Though outwardly we are wasting away, yet inwardly we are being renewed day by day" (2 Cor. 4:16).

🌿 🌿 🌿 🌿 🌿

Pieces: Can We Ever Get Them Together?

If our happiness—our fulfillment, is so dependent upon outward circumstances, what happens when those circumstances change?

This is a question asked by Glaphre Gilliland, a physically challenged Christian author. In her book, *When the Pieces Don't Fit*, God makes the difference as she struggles with the disappointment of not receiving physical healing.[1] She tells how her disabilities brought her to a meaningful relationship with the Lord. Wholeness from the average human standpoint means a perfect physical body. Sometimes we who have physical challenges tend to concentrate upon everything working and looking right, but Glaphre finds the real meaning of wholeness through God's Word. She learns how to pray and depends upon God for the true meaning of obedience.

What's with this pile of puzzle pieces we see all jumbled up in our world? Our physical body doesn't function perfectly. We feel pain that even an aspirin will not stop. We apply one relief device after another. If we keep trying, finally, we find physical relief, and we sigh with thankfulness. The pieces that seem to bring us physical comfort often

---

[1] Glaphre Gilliand is author of *When the Pieces Don't Fit* and *Talking With God*

come from outward sources, only to have the illness return. Perhaps we resist the management or cure of these spiritual puzzle pieces.

Joni Erickson Tada, the well-known author who has been paralyzed her entire adult life, says that there must be a frame for the puzzle pieces to fit together. She says the frame needed for spiritual brokenness is Jesus Christ. The Lord Jesus is like the completed edge around the picture of our life, and filling in the middle is not easy. At least she says there's a reference point. Life's complications are difficult to understand, and so are portions of God's Word. We keep going back to it, prayerfully reading it, until it makes sense.[2]

David Ring, an evangelist, says it was through his physical struggles that he found a true relationship with the Lord Jesus. He admits he "talks funny" and "walks funny." Without cerebral palsy he would have never searched for ways to put the inward jumble of his life together. As many of us who are physically challenged, he found that wholeness in Christ comes as we try to get the middle pieces within the puzzle frame (Jesus Christ) to fit. Only God can make us whole, put the pieces together, and bring us joy unspeakable and full of glory. Our victory is in Jesus.

Paul said, "Three times I pleaded with the Lord to take it (a thorn in his flesh) away from me. But he said to me, 'My grace is sufficient for you, for my power is made perfect in weakness'" (2 Cor. 12:8-9).

Ring says that God can make lemonade out of anybody's lemon. "Give God a lemon and watch how much lemonade He squeezes from it,"[3] he said while delivering a sermon.

A tart, sour lemon changes into sweet, refreshing lemonade when we give it to Jesus. Our painful, weak bodies that

2   Joni Erickson Tada is an author and speaker
3   David Ring is an evangelist and public speaker.

challenge us, remind us of a perfect God who can make us whole because of it, not in spite of it.

❧ ❧ ❧ ❧ ❧

My Heart Keeps Singing

Growing up, there was constantly a song in my heart and on my lips. In my early teens, I enjoyed walking alone through a wooded area in front of our home in Arkansas. In the fall of the year, the smell of trees and dying grass reached my nostrils, and the brown crisp leaves crunched under my feet. Sometimes they crackled and popped setting off my creative juices to make up words for a new song. If the lyrics of a familiar tune did not fit my mood, I would make up my own. After all, nobody was around to hear me or to squelch my joy. Words came easily.

At the expense of others, I often went about humming or singing whatever was on my mind. Working as a private secretary to an executive in Fort Worth, Texas, when I was twenty-seven, I discovered that it was possible to break the habit of constantly singing in public places. I was unaware of the annoyance my singing was causing until the day I slipped into the office of my boss and placed some letters, which I had transcribed for him on his desk. He thanked me.

I stopped my joyful noise long enough to give a cheerful, "You're welcome," and immediately resumed my singing. Just before I swished out the door he added in his Texas drawl, "Oh yes, Rachel, you can stay, but that sing'n has to go. Save it for church."

What a put down! I burned with embarrassment, but then I did some thinking. An executive office was not the place for my voice lessons. Since I loved my job and the people with whom I worked, I disciplined myself and confined my special favors to my home and church. Since then, I have been grateful for that "put down."

I've been singing since the time I could talk, my mother said. In college I took music and voice lessons, as well as choir directing. I was not a bad soprano, and I could handle other voice ranges.

Until 1970, I couldn't imagine not being able to sing. A stroke attacked my vocal chords. As I recuperated, I enrolled at Butler University in Indianapolis for therapy. The refresher course in voice slowly brought me back to a soprano. My instructor was very pleased when I finally reached above the alto range. This was an encouragement, for my goal was to sing again in a soprano voice range and to solo again.

Singing was the joy of my life, and I acquired enough courage to sing a solo one Sunday morning when the regular soloist failed to show up for worship. I volunteered to fill in for her. Of course, I would sing a familiar song, one I had sung many times. About halfway through it my voice cracked, disappeared, and I could not retrieve it. I lost it! The words would not come out. I excused myself and asked for a congregational hymn. When I told my instructor that week what had happened, he advised, "Just don't do them any more favors yet, Mrs. Wilfong."

I agreed, no more favors, but no one told me I couldn't sing to the rhythm of pots and pans in my kitchen. Although I was the choir director, I refused to sing too loudly after that. In fact, I refused to sing loud enough for anyone sitting near me to hear. I will never stop singing. Only when I am alone, will I sing aloud. No one can stop me from singing in my heart. You see, my singing is biblical, as King David said, "Sing to the Lord a new song; sing to the Lord, all the earth. Sing to the Lord, praise his name; proclaim his salvation day after day" (Ps. 96:1-2). In Ephesians 5:19, Paul said we should sing and make music in our hearts to the Lord. David said we should make a joyful noise unto the Lord.

Little by little, Polymyalgia trickled into my chest muscles. My voice was anything but beautiful. Since the vocal chords needed rest, my doctor advised me that it was time to give up teaching and public speaking. Giving up the church school class of young parents was most difficult. I turned to the Lord for strength. It was as though the words He spoke to Paul came clearly to me: "My grace is sufficient for you" (2 Cor. 12:9). Accepting His grace, I resigned. His grace has been enough. He has provided a way, and it took only a few weeks for me to completely let go. I've found wonderful things to sing about as I turn to handcrafts and writing for publication.

My heart continues to sing wherever I am. God provided replacements for me in every position I had to give up. If I have learned anything since I became physically challenged, it was that I am dispensable. God always provides a substitute, and I praise Him for His daily presence. I keep on singing. As I sing this song I wrote, I am never alone.

> I love to be alone with God,
> When it's just the two of us.
> He walks and talks with me
> Without a lot of fuss.
> His Word has so much power,
> To strengthen me each day.
> It puts a song in my heart,
> And drives discomfort away.
> His promise to me is true,
> He said His burden is light.
> If I turn it over to Him,
> Everything will be all right.
> I gave Him the Good News Class,

And I gave up speaking, too.
He has made my burden lighter,
As He shows me things I can do.
So I sing my song of praise,
As I take a day at a time;
Resting in His precious Love,
Fitting Him into each rhyme.[4]

The joy of the Lord is my strength. As John the Baptist said, "A man can receive only what is given him from heaven . . . . I am not the Christ but am sent ahead of him. The bride belongs to the bridegroom. The friend who attends the bridegroom waits and listens for him, and is full of joy when he hears the bridegroom's voice. That joy is mine, and it is now complete. He must become greater; I must become less" (John 3:27-30).

---

[4] Poem by Rachel Wilfong

5
Fruit of the Spirit

ove. We hear the word used to express our feelings toward
anything and anybody. For the past three decades the word
has been used to relate to sex, favorite foods, a piece of
jewelry, or a trip abroad. Anything that *feels good* is love.
Talk show hosts allow shouting matches between family members who are trying to prove their love. The fine line between hate and love challenges us to know the difference.
What does love mean?

Does it mean, "not having to say I'm sorry?" How can
we obtain love and know the difference between love and
passion?

At a time in my life when I was struggling to find love in
my heart for someone who was unlovable, I discovered unconditional love. Since God is love, the appropriate place to
find what I sought was in His Word. A serious truth in 1
John lunged at me. John spoke to me as a friend, "Love comes
from God."

"Ah, yes," I thought, "I can draw love from the source of love. God is love."

Dear friends, let us love one another, for love comes from God. Everyone who loves has been born of God and knows God. Whoever does not love does not know God, because God is love. This is how God showed his love among us; He sent his one and only Son into the world that we might live through him. This is love: not that we loved God, but he loved us and sent his Son as an atoning sacrifice for our sins. Dear friends, since God so loved us, we also ought to love one another. No one has ever seen God; but if we love each other, God lives in us and his love is made complete in us. We know that we live in him and he in us, because he has given us of his Spirit. And we have seen and testify that the Father has sent his Son to be the Savior of the world. If anyone acknowledges that Jesus is the Son of God, God lives in him and he in God. And so we know and rely on the love God has for us. *God is love. Whoever lives in love lives in God, and God in him.* (I John 4:7-16)

Pondering those words, I asked myself a question. What about loving one another? Did that mean everybody? If so, then I had a problem. My personal soul searching began with a piece of paper and a pen. I made a list of people with whom I had problems loving. Startled at what I had written, I laid my head over on the list and prayed.

"Father, it's hard — help me with my feelings! We are talking about unconditional love here, Lord, and I simply don't have it for these people."

I poured out my heart to Him. Past experiences swirled around me in Technicolor. Relationships with people had gone sour, and now a very special little person needed my love, and so did her mother.

Because this was my daughter's second child out of wed-
lock, I was hurt, angry, and I had been unable to forgive her.
Worst of all, I was finding it very difficult to love the child.

We adopted our eldest daughter when she was almost
twelve. The few years she had with us were not enough to
redeem her from a dysfunctional childhood. I came to the
point that I thought everything she chose to do was out of
rebellion and was meant to hurt me personally. Now, the time
had come when we would be seeing her, and I didn't really
want to see her or have anything to do with the child. Conviction burned within me. I cried in repentance to God and
asked Him to forgive me and give me unconditional love for
that tiny baby and her mother. I held back nothing as I wept
bitterly over my sinful attitude. I felt His warm presence and
forgiveness, but how would I feel when we would come face
to face? How would I feel toward the baby?

As my husband drove toward Indianapolis where our
daughter lived, I prayed all the way. The moment of truth
came when we turned into her driveway. I was struggling. I
wasn't sure how I felt, but I knew I had asked the right person for help. Ready or not, I must face my daughter.

The screen door of her next-door neighbor opened. Katy
had seen us drive up. She came through the door with her
baby cradled in a little pumpkin seat, as it was called in the
seventies. She walked slowly toward me, spoke to me, and
extended the child toward me. I can remember the anxious
expression on her face, as well as the uncertainty. I'm sure
she was wondering if I would be glad to see them. Would her
mother accept her little one?

A warm blanket of love flooded my entire body as I
reached out to take the child. I tried to hold back the tears. I
touched the tiny little baby girl's hand, stroked her little round

face, and I knew right then and there that God had given me that love for which I had asked. Through the tears I saw the expression on my daughter's face change into a pleasant smile. What she had hoped for had happened. Her mother wasn't angry with her anymore. After a short visit with them we left. All the way home I thought I would explode with praise to God. The burden I had been carrying for so long was gone. He had turned my sorrow into joy.

God's commandments to us were never given without His promise to help us keep them. I was to love others as He had loved me. He promised if I would ask anything of Him, He would do it. Out of somewhere surfaced that love. I felt Him draw me closer to Him in memory of how much He loved me. In reviewing His commandments and my response to them, my heart was filled with gratitude, and His love flooded my soul.

This experience was the beginning of a wholesome understanding of God's love. The Holy Spirit speaks to my heart again and again, reminding me of how important the healing of bad relationships is, that it can only come through prayer. With confidence in a loving, caring Father I can ask Him for a refreshing filling of the Holy Spirit to help me love the unlovable.

Since God is love, He alone can give love. If at any time I feel barren of this gift, I turn to Him again for help.

> Love is patient, love is kind. It does not envy, it does not boast, it is not proud. It is not rude, it is not self-seeking, it is not easily angered, it keeps no record of wrongs. Love does not delight in evil but rejoices with the truth. It always . . . perseveres. Love never fails. (1 Cor. 13:4-8a)

PEACE V. TURMOIL

Merideth and I enjoy relaxing after meals. The double windows in our home provide a ringside seat to view God's creation.

One spring morning two young rabbits played mischievously on our lawn. Face to face, they hunkered down, daring each other to make the first move. With a twitch of their ears, they took aim. One jumped high off the ground; the other dashed under him. They repeated their acrobatic game for several minutes. They were so free and comfortable with each other. Our pet dog, Frisky, was no threat to them. Soon they separated. One hopped briskly into the grassy field beside our lawn. The other disappeared behind the little storage barn.

It had only been a few days since I had seen a robin and a starling fighting. The relationship between the feathered creatures was anything but friendly. I noticed that I was not the only spectator to this violent sideshow. Approximately three feet from them was a small rabbit, sitting on its haunches, watching the combat. The two birds moved swiftly in their fight. With a quick jerk, the rabbit turned his head each time they moved.

We could learn a lesson from the animals and birds. Each scene reminded me of people. The rabbits were playful and unafraid. The birds were unwilling to give an inch in their fight for their rights. Some people are constantly fighting over or about something. Others are content and happy, getting along well with others. Have you ever been around someone who had nothing but problems? They pepper their conversation with life's problems. If you get an opportunity to jump in with a positive word, they extinguish your voice immediately with buts and ifs. It is as though they are trying to convince you that a solution is impossible.

What causes fights and quarrels among us? James, the apostle, seemed to think that they are caused by our own desires (James 4:1-3). The battle is within us. We want something, but we don't get it. We kill and covet, but we cannot have what we want. We quarrel and fight. We do not have because we do not ask God. When we ask, we do not receive, because we ask with wrong motives. We may use that which we receive on our personal pleasures.

"A heart at peace gives life to the body, but envy rots the bones," says Proverbs 14:30. We can choose to seek peace. James wrote, "Humble yourselves before the Lord, and he will lift you up" (James 4:10). It is also by choice that we focus our attention upon ourselves and strive against others. James tells us in James 3:17-18 to ask for wisdom from heaven, which is pure, peace loving, considerate, submissive, full of mercy and good fruit, impartial, and sincere. Peacemakers who sow peace raise a harvest of righteousness.

I can continue in turmoil like the birds, or I can play happily at peace like the rabbits. I pray for wisdom in every decision I must make in life.

❧ ❧ ❧ ❧ ❧

Snooty Birds and Uninvited Guests

Behind the parsonage in Indiana where our bird feeder stood, were two beautiful doves. They were peacefully feasting on the food that had fallen to the ground. A sojourner moved in to take his share. However, a squatter, who had claimed the turf and the food from the feeder, didn't think much of the uninvited guest. The flippant bird raised his head, came down on the bum with a firm peck, took another bite and pecked again. The intruder got the message and took flight.

It reminded me of the way God's children sometimes act. He has prepared for us a bountiful supply of food. How dare anyone come uninvited to share it with us? We have claimed this little turf, the food provided, and we expect everyone else should likewise find their own. Like the doves, after we peck others away, we consume our gifts from God. We leave only the crumbs to those less fortunate.

Lessons of life are not all learned from my window. During the Christmas season one year, I had an unexpected visitor. A little boy about eight came unannounced. I enjoy children, but it wasn't the best time for company to pop in. The little fellow was warm and friendly and moved right into the kitchen, where I was preparing a meal. I delayed dinner while he asked questions about everything in sight. Was he going to force me to invite him to share our dinner for two? If I invited him to eat, then my husband and I would have to share our piece of meat. When I saw that he was perched in the extra chair to stay, I asked him if he had eaten. The answer I anticipated came. He had not.

"I am not really hungry," he assured me.

"Are you sure?" I asked. I was relieved when he added, "But I'll have a glass of tea."

When I placed a dish of bright, green broccoli topped with creamy cheese sauce on the table, his eyes lit up. He took a deep breath, expressed a sigh of approval with "I *luv* broccoli with cheese sauce on it."

I reached for another plate. We prayed, shared our meat with him, and passed him the broccoli. He wasn't kidding. He loved broccoli! He was very well mannered, said "thank you," and "yes, please," as we ate dinner. When he had finished, he helped me with the dishes, politely thanked me again for the dinner and went on his way. As I watched him leave the drive, I was overcome with guilt. How frustrated I was when he showed up. I had wrestled with the decision to share our meal made for two. Our little guest went away happily, and we had plenty of food for the three of us. I asked God to forgive me for my selfish attitude.

I remembered the doves. They didn't provide the bird feed that had fallen to the ground. They had not worked for it. The food on my table was a gift from God. How dare any of us feel that we have a right to decide if a little boy should share our dinner?

The little sojourner frequented our home after that. As we became more acquainted with him, we learned that he was mistreated in his home. How glad we were that we shared our meal with him. This incident changed my attitude. I've learned if I praise God for what I have, and if I share the gifts He has given me, I avoid being snooty and troubled at a challenge to entertain strangers.

> Keep on loving each other as brothers. Do not forget to entertain strangers, for by so doing some people have entertained angels without knowing it. Remember those in prison as if you were their fellow prisoners, and those who are *mistreated as if you yourselves were suffering.* (Heb. 13:1-3)

🌿 🌿 🌿 🌿 🌿

FORGIVENESS

"I can forgive but I can't forget." Sound familiar? Can we really forget an injury toward us? Where's the limit?

To forget means to be unable to think of or recall; to fail to become mindful of at the proper time. To forgive is to give up resentment; to grant relief from payment of.

I once heard an emotional conversation between siblings concerning the way their father had disciplined them when they were growing up. True, theirs' was a valid discussion. As they recalled their childhood, hate, anger, and resentment all oozed out with trembling words. The sister and brother are both wonderful Christians and seek God's will in their lives daily.

Can a person ever get rid of the hurts, the memories of abuse, as they grow older? Can a battered wife ever forgive that which has happened to her? *Unger's Bible Dictionary* says this about forgiveness: "Forgiveness is the most widely misunderstood doctrine of the Scripture. It is not to be confused with human forgiveness which merely remits a penalty of charge."[1]

In the Old Testament the priest made atonement for the people, and their sins were forgiven. Such forgiveness served as a covering of sins (Deut. 21:8-9). God would deal, finally, with sin through the death of His Son. The operation of such forgiveness is called "salvation." The unbeliever's forgiveness comes as he responds in simple faith in Christ.

A believer's standing in Christ is complete. He is perfected forever in Christ. When a believer sins, the Holy Spirit convicts him of the wrong. He must seek forgiveness for that which has summoned the operation of the Holy Spirit in that instance. In order to obtain relief, he must be chastised by the Father, and in order to be forgiven, he must confess his sin before the Father. Such a confession brings forgiveness and restores one to fellowship (1 Cor. 11:31,32; 1 John 1:9).

Is it any wonder that there are 95 references in the back of my Bible concerning forgiveness? Jesus never asks us to do anything that we cannot do. This is a tough one! Jesus knows

---

[1] Unger, Merrill F., *Unger's Bible Dictionary*, (Chicago, IL: Moody Bible Institute of Chicago, Third Edition 1975) p. 377

forgiveness. He forgave those who put him to death while he was dying. He died for us when we were yet sinners, and instructs us that if we do not forgive, we are not forgiven.

How can we experience forgiveness? I asked God for a forgiving spirit. No one could help me but He who forgave me. When disobedient children hurt their parents, it often results in anger. I was once angry and found forgiveness a hard thing. So I asked God to create in me a new heart. He did, and I forgave.

What about forgiving someone no longer alive? For years, my heart burned with memories of some unpleasant experiences I suffered as a child. I tried so hard to rid myself of the judgment toward the one who was responsible, but I could not. Like a bolt of lightening, Mark 11:25 struck my hurting heart: "And when you stand praying, if you hold anything against anyone, forgive him, so that your Father in heaven may forgive you."

Since my perpetrator was no longer alive, the reconciliation had to be between my Lord and me. How could I forgive a person who couldn't seek my forgiveness? God's promise was not altered by my lack of understanding. I surrendered all my feelings to God and asked Him to "forgive my trespasses as I forgave those who trespass against me," and to give me a kind and forgiving heart for this person. Whether the person was dead or alive, I could not continue the hatred and anger. Each day I am amazed that even if I think unholy thoughts, I feel the continuous forgiveness of the Father. Since God gave me the spirit to forgive, I am no longer in torment. I know that we will meet again and our thoughts will be pure toward one another.

"What about forgetting?" you may ask.

I remember the pain, but as I review my past without the old anger, resentment, and hate, I know that the memory serves only to remind me of that for which I was forgiven and that I have forgiven. It doesn't particularly mean I don't remember the abuse I suffered at the hands of another; I remember without all the hurt and fear.

Forgiving and forgetting doesn't always take place immediately upon asking, but the process does begin a sincere desire to be "kind and compassionate to one another, forgiving . . ." (Eph. 4:32). Merrill Unger writes that, "The believer who belongs to this age is exhorted to be kind unto other believers, and unbelievers as well, tenderhearted and forgiving to one another as God for Christ's sake hath forgiven you.[2]

A mind forgets. A heart forgives. The basis of my plea for forgiveness is that I, myself, have been so graciously forgiven. Therefore, I can forgive and forget. I have learned much from my daughter, Gwen. In a discussion about forgiveness and forgetting she said, "If our minds forget, then we won't remember enough to correct a wrong."

Well said, my beloved daughter.

---

[2] Ibid.

6
Family Holidays

To sing *Thanksgiving Day* is to relive fond memories.

Over the river and through the wood,
To Grandfather's house we go;
The Horse knows the way
To carry the sleigh
Through the white and drifted snow.

Over the river and through the wood—
Oh, how the wind does blow!
It stings the toes
And bites the nose,
As over the ground we go.

Over the river and through the wood,
To have a first-rate play.

Hear the bells ring,
"Ting-a-ling-ding!"
Hurrah for Thanksgiving Day!

Over the river and through the wood,
Trot fast, my dapple-gray!
Spring over the ground,
Like a hunting-hound!
For this is Thanksgiving Day.

Over the river and through the wood,
And straight through the barnyard gate.
We seem to go extremely slow—
It is so hard to wait!

Over the river and through the wood—
Now Grandmother's cap I spy!
Hurrah for the fun!
Is the pudding done?
Hurrah for the pumpkin pie!
(Lydia Maria Child, 1802-1880[1])

Uncle Floyd's new house was nestled back in the woodland in central Arkansas. On a Thanksgiving long ago, we traveled to uncle Floyd's, where we would see my little redheaded, Irish grandfather. Since there was no real road from our house to my uncle's, my father made a one-horse sleigh. A narrow roadway had been cleared through the young saplings, trees, and brush. Only horse-drawn wagons could get through that wet, winding trail.

---

[1] Lydia Marie Child, author

It had been a chilly, rainy season. As we slid swiftly through the wood, "Thanksgiving Day" was the perfect song to sing. "Over the river and through the wood . . . ." There we were, five kids all bundled up, snuggled close to mother for warmth while daddy stood up holding the tight reigns to guide old Dolly, our faithful horse. The load was a bit challenging for her, but she served her master well.

Our "river" was water that filled the deep ruts and covered the trail. I can see the sleigh runners parting the muddy liquid, swirling sheets of it into the brush and trees to each side. It didn't matter that our "white and drifted snow" never arrived by Thanksgiving Day. Our imagination turned that flying water into the white stuff, and our song kept us in the mood. As far as we were concerned, there could have been falling snow and a winding river. Our horse sprang over the ground like a hunting hound accompanying our laughter and song with the "clackity clop" of her hoofs. How joyful we were, in spite of splashing drops of water that swished into our singing mouths. The closed gate to my uncle's barnyard served as a conductor's wand, bringing the cheerful symphony to an abrupt halt.

When we, one by one, rolled off the sleigh, we didn't see grandmother in her cap. She had died when I was an infant. Those who talked about her kept the memories alive. Granddaddy stood watching as we approached him. The smell of wood burning in the old wood fireplace and the wood range drew us straight to the kitchen. Roast turkey in the oven, its aromas mixed with the sweet smell of pies and cakes, seem to fill my nostrils even now as I reflect upon those happy times. Sounds of children's playful voices, and laughter from the adults still linger as I type this.

A sweet, joyful spirit existed among the members of my mother's family. To this day, I cannot recall any time when there was friction between any of them. One almost forgot which child belonged to whom at those festive family gatherings, where such loyalty and caring were demonstrated. Miles and death have separated me from uncles, aunts, and cousins, but this song, "Thanksgiving Day," brings us together in my mind as I pretend I am with them again, and I thank God for my heritage during the Thanksgiving season.

The Christmas Nightmare

Several weeks before Christmas 1983, excitement mounted. This was to be our best Christmas ever. Now that Deanette lived with us, her mother and brother would be arriving mid-afternoon on Christmas Eve. Gwen and her family were expected on Christmas Day. A turkey dinner with all the trimmings was in the making. What excitement!

That all changed on Christmas Eve. A telephone message came from Annette, Deanette's mother, and her arrival would be delayed. The winter storm, which had already dumped snow and ice on the highways, was causing more havoc. Roads were closing, and traveling was getting risky. She would still be here, but it would be evening before she could make it.

Emotions were running scared. Moods started to change. This was the first time Deanette would be with her mother and brother at our house since she was very small. Surely nothing would happen now. Her mother was to pick up her brother in Peru, Indiana, and an early arrival would have given them more time to be together.

In the meantime, another telephone call came. It was from Little Rock, Arkansas. Merideth's mother had suffered a severe heart attack the day before and wasn't expected to live. Bad news was filtering into the parsonage. Annette finally called to say she was indeed stranded. Highway 31 was closed. She could not get out of Peru. When was it going to stop? What else could happen? Disappointment built up by the moment. It seemed that all we could do was sit almost paralyzed, waiting for the phone to ring.

The worst news we could receive came by mid-afternoon. Mother Wilfong died at 2:30 p.m. We would have to set things in motion and try to get to Little Rock. We called Gwen in Three Rivers, Michigan. They would get to us as soon and as safely as they could in order to travel south with us on Christmas Day.

How terrible for Deanette! Her mother couldn't make it. Deanette couldn't go with us, because her father had made arrangements to come for her as soon as he could travel during the holiday. A serious decision must be made. While she was crushed under such disappointing events, turning our plans upside down, I saw her snap out of it when the parents of her friend, Denise Seals, became her refuge. Deanette's father would come for her as soon as possible, but he couldn't make it until after Christmas. She could stay with her friend until he came.

I've always been amazed at Deanette's ability to overcome, but she had fourteen years of practice. Her childhood had been like a roller coaster, and she had learned to cope with adjustments. By the time we left her on Christmas Day, she was handling things well and looking forward to seeing her father.

Heading south on Christmas Day left much to be desired. We had recently purchased a handicap van and this would be its first long trip in cold weather. We found ourselves traveling in minus zero weather with a faulty heater. It was bitter cold. Four adults and two children snuggled together, trying to keep warm. Our blankets and covers helped the passengers, but they were no help to Merideth while he drove.

As if the cold wasn't enough, we were getting hungry. If we could just find a warm restaurant with some hot coffee and chocolate, that would help. We passed one closed cafe after another. "Closed for the Holiday," the signs said. The words seemed to shout at us as our eyes searched for a sign of life and food along the highway.

Ah! Finally, late in the afternoon we spotted vapor oozing from vent pipes. It was a restaurant. Somebody was alive in there. We could see that inside there was steam on the windows — the most welcome sight of the day! A comfort stop and the food helped us. We slipped back into our covers and drove a few miles before the sun started to go down, and then we began to get very cold. Aware of the ice-covered highways and streets ahead, we stopped in Memphis to call Little Rock. Relatives advised us that everything was covered with ice, and an alternate route to enter North Little Rock was suggested. We were warned of the ice we would run into at Forest City, and then it would be very hazardous and slippery traveling the rest of the way.

And that's the way it was! Cautiously, Merideth drove while we prayed. We arrived, frozen stiff but safely, at the Wilfong home in North Little Rock about midnight. It took the rest of the night for us to thaw. A long, difficult week was yet to come. The funeral, which was scheduled to take place on Tuesday, was postponed because of ice. A private memorial was held with only the family present at the funeral home. Merideth spoke to the family, and Dave, our son-in-law, helped him with the reading of the Scriptures. Since I was stranded with my wheelchair and could not go, Gwen stayed with me at Mother Wilfong's house.

The scheduled funeral for the public was held on Thursday, with the graveside service set for Friday morning, ninety miles north of Little Rock. Since it was on our way home, we were prepared to start home immediately from the cemetery.

After a cold trip back home, all day and nearly all night, our home was a welcome sight. It was three o'clock Saturday morning. The parsonage was toast warm. Nobody wasted any time hitting the covers. We felt so safe, so blessed to be alive and to have a comfortable parsonage to come home to. Gwen's family got a few hours sleep, and left Saturday morning to get back to their home and church at Three Rivers.

We learned from the Seals family that Deanette's father had come for her, and she was spending Christmas vacation with him. Christmas packages were still unopened until January 8. Annette finally was able to come for Christmas dinner and a gift-exchange party.

Isn't it strange how awful things seem for a while, and how quickly we as Christians can forget? Thank God for His almighty care for us! It's all like a dream now, and I wonder how it is with those who have no Christian faith by which to live.

Deanette overcame her *bad time* extremely well and had a good visit with her father and family in Rensselaer, Indiana.

I was so grateful for our church family. So many of them helped us during that difficult time. Their prayers, financial extras, and wonderful messages in cards and flowers told us how much they cared. God took care of us during that Christmas nightmare.

꙲ ꙲ ꙲ ꙲ ꙲

Gifts

It was Christmas Day 1985. The traditional Hungarian Christmas bread, topped with sweet transparent glaze, colorful candied fruits, and nuts, made an enticing centerpiece on the oval-shaped dining table. The aroma of coffee filled the parsonage. Beautiful, carefully wrapped presents covered a third of the living room around the Christmas tree. Our daughter, Gwen, her husband and two daughters, filtered into the kitchen one-by-one. Annette, our third daughter, and her friend, Gregg, followed them.

In no time the beautiful centerpiece was disfigured. A second pot of coffee was brewing, and it was time to open gifts. As usual, that took the rest of the morning. Excitement started to wind down after each gift had been examined. "What's for dinner?" echoed through the house. Gifts had been set aside as appetites became more important. Dinner was planned. On the menu was prime rib roast, ham, home-made dinner rolls, candied yams, green beans, and tossed salad. What, no turkey? Not this time. Annette had baked mincemeat pies the night before. The Jell-O bell, which I had tackled, turned out perfectly. The table was set with new china, a gift from our granddaughter, Deanette, and her grandpa.

Annette and Gregg had to leave early after dinner. Gwen and I stood and looked at the kitchen, then plunged into the task of cleaning up.

When the last dish was put away, I wandered through the house, overwhelmed. Clothing, trinkets, and toys covered the floor and furniture.

"Gifts," I said to Gwen. "Look at them."

Gwen helped me make room for seating as we discussed our appreciation for each one. We talked of how exciting it was to open presents and watch expressions of each person as they uncovered mysteries. We recognized the love behind each gift that was specially chosen for each of us.

Yet, sometimes gifts seem to snuff out the real meaning of Christmas. The ultimate gift, God's Son, brought peace to the hearts of men. That peace is real and necessary for our daily living throughout the year.

Sitting there, I pondered the words of Jesus, "Peace I leave with you, my peace I give you. I do not give to you as the world gives. Do not let your hearts be troubled and do not be afraid" (John 14:27). "I have told you these things, so that in me you may have peace. In this world you will have trouble. But take heart! I have overcome the world" (John 16:33). These words are from the Prince of Peace.

"Are you OK, mother?" Gwen's voice interrupted my thoughts.

"Oh, yes, I'm fine, very fine," I replied.

ఠ ఠ ఠ ఠ ఠ

Christmas Sounds Linger

It was Monday, December 26, 1988, the day after Christmas. Squeals from the mouths of babes penetrated throughout the parsonage. Sounds of banging doors told us the grandchildren were having fun. Now and then a cold draft found its way through the entry door left ajar. Voices of parents, grandparents, aunts, and uncles catching up on the news did not interrupt the teenagers in a nearby bedroom. Sounds of laughter expressed their thrills and excitement of growing up.

Christmas sounds linger on. Ah yes! I can hear them now, "I'm hungry, Grandma." Their passion for food was accompanied by their footsteps as they chased each other through the house. Above the background of hissing televisions were the clanging of pots and pans and the rattle of dishes.

It was difficult to sneak in a little Christmas music from the radio or record player. Noisy? Yes, but in the midst of it there was tranquillity brought on by a special love of the one whose birthday we were celebrating.

Warm tears rolled down my cheeks as I observed the cluttered living room. Blurred bits of Christmas gift wrapping, mangled boxes, and a ribbon here and there, unfolded years gone by. Another year is past, and the children and grandchildren were gone. Only memories remained in a very quiet parsonage.

Alone, Merideth and I sat quietly, discussing our love for our four daughters. Mixed emotions surfaced as we spoke of those who were absent. Our hearts were filled with the love of God. Calling each by name added comfort to our feelings.

A special friend of our family wrote a scripture on a Christmas card: "So do not fear, for I am with you; be not dismayed, for I am your God; I will strengthen you and help you; I will uphold you with my righteous right hand" (Isa. 41:10). I memorized the passage of scripture and placed it on the refrigerator door to remind me how faithful God is.

Throughout the year lingering sounds come as a reminder of God's Son, who came to give us the joy of them. Lingering Christmas sounds, yes, and how sweet those sounds.

7

New Life in Jesus

It was in the summer of 1978. What may have appeared to be a *bed and breakfast* was the parsonage. Unlike any other parsonage in which we had lived, it was located so that our friends and relatives from across the United States could find their way to us. A bus load of young people with Campus Crusade had invaded the town. The Sunday evening music concert was over. Each student had found his or her host for the night and was settling in. The college girls we were hosting were making themselves at home with other guests who had arrived that day. A couple and four children were adding to the chatter that filled the house. One of the students was a daughter of some friends in Texas. We were catching up on the family news, while spreading our hospitality to include all of our guests.

This story is about Betty, the mother of the four children. We met Betty and Dan (not their real names), when they were in the Air Force stationed at Bunker Hill, Indiana.

Dan was a faithful member of our church in Bunker Hill. Dan had difficulty getting Betty to join him, but he refused to let her interfere with his attendance. His prayer requests always included Betty, who was not a believer. With a smile, he would say, "I'm not giving up on her."

Dan's love for Betty, and his faith and prayers for her, were honored. The change in Betty came when she attended a youth workshop I was teaching on Sunday evenings. It was an endeavor to train the youth of our church about winning others to Christ. Betty was more comfortable with young people than she was with adults. Like a simple innocent child, she sat through each session with Dan. They were very young and in love, and Betty wanted to be near her husband.

A few sessions of the workshop were given to self-examination of our relationship with Christ. Each student was encouraged to choose a friend or relative who needed to believe in Christ. They would pray for them daily and during the sessions.

One evening of the workshop was set aside to practice what we had learned. Since I had fractured my foot and was in a cast, the group was organized at the parsonage and "sent out" on their assignment. We would, by appointment, visit those whose names were on our prayer list. Two people would visit. An experienced soul winner would accompany a student. Betty invited a team to visit her, and requested Dan's presence. Therefore, assigning our youth leader to accompany him was appropriate.

Betty's new life began that evening. She was one of the few who said yes to Jesus. The teams were scheduled to report at the parsonage when they were finished. Bursting with excitement over her newfound faith, Betty charged in ahead of the group to tell the good news. Her spiritual growth from that night forward was nonstop. Her commitment to Christ touched others wherever she went.

It was getting late and our houseguests were disappearing one by one as they retired for the evening. Betty and I talked into the late hours. She shared the tragic story of how she had lost two small children in a fatal fire. She had grown stronger in her faith. God's grace saw her through the experience and gave her four more children.

She reflected upon the past. The accident happened when Dan was stationed in Texas. Their home was a doublewide mobile home on the military base. Betty had put the two children to bed for their afternoon nap and was next door, a few feet away. She kept her eyes on their trailer while her two children slept. Suddenly, right before her, the trailer exploded. Both children died in that explosion.

They visited us in Indianapolis shortly after the funeral, and I remember Betty's expression of faith when she said, "The children are safe with the Lord." She chuckled through tears when she added, "God has blessed me with fertility. He will give us more children."

"*God certainly did give them more children,*" I was thinking. I had just helped her put four bundles-of-energy to bed.

Christ made a difference in Betty's life. The explosion that took four-year-old Stacy and two-year-old Mike called for undying faith. Like Job of the Old Testament, she had withstood the test. She and her husband knew in whom they placed their trust. Coming from non-Christian homes, it was important to each of them that Christ would become known to their families. Tears filled my eyes as I gazed at the four blurred figures before me. If God can bring such blessings and peace to Betty and Dan, He can do it for other parents.

I prayed that God would give me teaching skills so that the forty young parents I taught could know Christ as Betty and Dan knew Him. Some of them had also experienced tragedy. Knowing that Christ makes the difference, I will continue to trust His words, "But I, when I am lifted up from the earth, will draw all men to myself" (John 12:32). My responsibility is to lift up Christ; He will do the drawing.

&& && && && &&

Karen Finds a New Life

My husband was pastor of a small church on the east side of Indianapolis in the seventies. The gay lifestyle was becoming more visible, cult and satanic worship were on the rise, and confused young people were making their way to the pastor's office for help.

A twenty-eight-year-old wife and mother was one of those who came for help. It was in the month of December 1975. Karen (not her real name) surrendered her life to Christ and was having difficulty with the transition. In her search for help, she found herself in Merideth's office at the church. I became involved when the parsonage telephone rang.

"Honey, would you please come over to the church?" Merideth said. His voice sounded anxious. "I have a young lady asleep on my office floor. I'll explain when you get here."

"I'll be right there," I replied, feeling a little curious as I hung up.

Quickly, I threw on my coat and made my way across the cold, paved parking lot to the church. Merideth was waiting for me outside his office. He immediately explained why Karen was there and told me what was going on.

The night before, at a Wednesday evening prayer meeting at a large church in the city, Karen had responded to an invitation. As in many churches, this one had assigned counselors to be available for those who made decisions. The lady who counseled Karen heard her confession and prayed with her. Karen was concerned about her ugly past and told her counselor that she came from a terribly abusive home, and that her life had been controlled by the devil. Seeing how fearful she was, the lady assured her that she was free of Satan. Now that Christ had come into her life, Satan would never bother her again.

To the contrary, Satan, whom Karen had worshipped in the past, tempted her to doubt, and was not going to let go easily. He was doing everything he could to cause her fear. Far greater trauma than Karen could understand overwhelmed her.

When she returned to her home after church, she went to bed but could not sleep. Satan tormented her throughout the night with his evil lies and accusations, tempting her to doubt her new birth. His forces filled her room with evil images. Confused and exhausted, she set out for help. When no one in her family could understand, she remembered that her sister, Darlene, was a new Christian, and went to her. The unbelieving members of her family had only made matters worse for her. In fact, they tried to convince her that she was losing her mind and they began making arrangements to have her committed. In a frantic search for help, she went to her sister. Darlene turned to her pastor, Merideth. She brought Karen to him, and after an introduction, left her in his office to tell her story.

Karen told of times when her mother literally took her by the hair of her head, swirling her around and tossing her down a flight of steps in her home. The harder she tried to rid herself of her haunting past, the more confused she became. Merideth sensed a heavy, suffocating, oppression surrounding them in the room. Not knowing exactly what else to do at the moment, he suggested that they call upon the

Lord in prayer. She agreed, and the Lord's model prayer began to flow from his lips.

"Father in heaven. Hallowed be thy name. Thy kingdom come, Thy will be done. . . ."

Karen fell on her knees beside him. Although she admitted later that she had never read or known the prayer, she spoke the words with him. When they came to "deliver us from evil," Karen suddenly collapsed in a solid clump upon the office floor. She began to writhe and contort as white froth oozed from her mouth. It was obvious to Merideth that God had heard their prayer for deliverance, and it must be what was happening right before his eyes.

Astonished, but calmly, he observed the scene at his feet. Feeling no urge to intrude, he just waited upon the Lord. Suddenly the resistance stopped. That altercation in Karen's new life was over, and she fell into a peaceful sleep. It was at this point that my awestruck husband called me and asked me to please come over to the church. He met me in the foyer outside his office and immediately began to explain to me why a beautiful lady was asleep on his office floor.

When he finished the story he suggested, "Let's let her sleep now. I thought it would be appropriate if you were here with me."

Between the office and where we stood was a large picture window. I stepped over to the window and peeped through the olive-green sheers that draped softly on the inside. In a fetal position on the floor was a sleeping beauty. She was about five-feet-four-inches tall and appeared to weigh approximately one hundred and ten pounds. Strands of long, tear-soaked, medium brown hair complimented her relaxed face.

"Come," Merideth said, "let's have some coffee while she sleeps."

Still slightly dazed over it all, I responded. "That's a good idea," and followed him down the flight of steps to the kitchen. While the coffee was brewing, we took cups from the cabinet. At the last drip we poured the fresh coffee and waited in the lounge outside the kitchen. We talked and prayed. An hour and a half later an attractive, light brunette stood in the doorway.

With a sleepy smile she said, "I really slept, didn't I?" She stretched and yawned, then drawled, "I feel much, much better."

Merideth turned to me, introduced the two of us and said, "Rae, this is Karen, Darlene's sister."

I acknowledged the introduction and offered her a cup of coffee. As she sipped the coffee, I noticed her hands trembled. She seemed a little apprehensive as she spoke.

"I'm not sure what happened in there, but I know something's happening to my life, and I know I belong to Jesus now." Her facial expression changed into puzzlement when she confessed, "I just don't understand why I have mixed feelings. How can I feel so secure and confused at the same time?" She fixed her soft, brown, inquiring eyes upon Merideth and waited for his response.

"Karen," he said. "You know when we prayed 'deliver us from evil,' in the office? Well, God heard us. You are being delivered from evil. The devil has had control over your life so long, and now he is fighting a losing battle. If he can't keep you, he doesn't want you to be at peace. He knows the Scripture, too. He knows that 'the one who is in you is greater than the one who is in the world' (1 John 4:4). The Holy Spirit of God is working in you, and the one who is in the world, Satan, is overcome in your life."

"I know the Ouija board has got me all messed up," Karen confessed. "I threw it away with all the other things."

She told more of her story. Her family was involved in satanic activities, and her mother was the leader. Her unbelieving family's threat to put her away did not daunt her faith in her new experience. They would not believe her when she insisted that she was not crazy. Her husband, Paul (not his real name), was supportive and wanted to help her. He just didn't understand. Paul, being an unbeliever, was not in tune with the spiritual battle within Karen.

> The man without the Spirit does not accept the things that come from the Spirit of God, for they are foolishness to him, and he cannot understand them, because they are spiritually discerned. (1 Cor. 2:14)

Since the beginning of her quest for peace, Karen's sleepless nights were taking a toll on her. She was afraid to go home and face another night of nightmares, but she had her family to think about.

Seeing that she was not yet alert, I asked, "Karen, do you think Paul would object if you stay with us a night or two? You need some physical rest, and we will try to help you overcome the fearful moments."

After a few seconds of silence, Karen responded to my suggestion. "Oh, that would be good. Would you call my husband and talk to him? Tell him what is happening. Tell him I am not crazy, and that I am going to be all right." She wrote down her telephone number and handed it to me.

"Of course," I said. I took the number and went to the office to make the call. I asked God for courage to speak as the phone rang.

A friendly voice answered the telephone. I introduced myself, told Paul where Karen was, and explained our interpretation of what was going on with his wife. When I suggested that she stay a few nights with us, he seemed relieved.

He was very cooperative and agreed that it might help for her to get some uninterrupted sleep.

"What can I do to help?" He offered.

"As a matter of fact, you can help," I replied. "If you will take care of the girls, Paul, we will take care of your wife." Then I tried to encourage him. "After Karen gets some rest, she will be able to think more clearly. If not, and we see that we cannot help her through this, we will recommend other professional help."

"That's fine," he said cheerfully.

The time was appropriate for me to ask Paul if he was a Christian. His answer was no, but he didn't mind if we helped his wife. Before I hung up, I gave him our phone number. When I saw Merideth standing beside me, I commented, "For a man who isn't a Christian, he's very helpful." With enthusiasm I added, "Wouldn't it be great if he would trust in the Lord?"

"Sure would," Merideth replied. "We've never had a situation quite like this one, have we?"

We rejoined Karen, and the three of us walked across the parking lot to the parsonage. Once inside, Karen chose to lie on the couch in the family room. While I went about my chores, I prayed that God would lead us through the hours ahead. Eating lunch was a problem for Karen, who wasn't very hungry. After a few bites she fell back onto the couch. I had to wonder how she would do during the night? Darkness came, hovering over the city.

Merideth and I agreed to take turns sitting near Karen. Bedtime triggered anxiety for our sleepless guest. She fired one question after another and talked about her past. The only thing we could do during that night was to prayerfully listen to her, read the Bible to her, and love her through the transition. As she awoke from her sporadic naps, she would sit up and look to see if one of us was in the rocker beside her.

"Please read from the Living Bible book some more." Her sleepy voice was that of a girl's, and like a child clinging to bedtime stories, she fought sleep.

I forced my eyelids to stay open as I read from John's Gospel. "For God loved the world so much that he gave his only Son so that anyone who believes in him shall not perish but have eternal life" (John 3:16 TLB). She absorbed the words like a soft sponge before falling asleep.

During the next day, Karen had some new experiences. For example, she said, "Oh, my goodness! I just remembered a friend of mine. I was so mean to her; I hurt her feelings. I wonder if I could call her and tell her I'm sorry?" Before I could respond to her question, she interrupted with, "Oh, she won't forgive me. She might even be really mad at me if I call her. No, I better not."

When later I heard the sound of the receiver as it settled onto the hook, I knew she had made the call.

"Guess what?" She raised her voice with excitement as she ran toward me. "She forgave me; she really did. She's not mad at me any more."

One surprise followed another. Before contacting each person with whom she had encountered personal conflicts, we prayed that God would give her strength to do what was right. Righteousness was prevailing.

Upon waking up from one of her short, daytime naps, Karen said, "Oh Rae, you know what? I just thought of something I took from the toy department in a store. It was only a little thing, but I did take it home with me. I stole it! Do you think they will think I am crazy if I return it?"

The Holy Spirit was definitely at work. Like a spotlight, He focused upon those things that had cluttered Karen's life.

She could no longer be happy until each wrong had been rectified. She responded to the Holy Spirit as He convicted her of all that was ungodly. He convicted her to return a Gideon Bible, which she had taken from a nearby hospital waiting room in the beginning of her search for the Lord. She was being made clean.

Jesus said of the Holy Spirit: "When he comes, he will convict the world of guilt in regard to sin and righteousness and judgment: in regard to sin, because men do not believe in me; in regard to righteousness, because I am going to the Father, where you can see me no longer; and in regard to judgment, because the prince of this world now stands condemned" (John 16:8-11).

It was obvious that Karen had become a new creature in Christ Jesus. She was a newborn adjusting to a new life. She was uncomfortable with her old life, and it was a traumatic transition.

> Therefore, if anyone is in Christ, he is a new creation; the old has gone, the new has come! All this is from God, who reconciled us to himself through Christ and gave us the ministry of reconciliation: that God was reconciling the world to himself in Christ, not counting men's sins against them. (2 Cor. 5:17-19)

When Nicodemus came to him at night, Jesus said, "I tell you the truth, unless a man is born again, he cannot see the kingdom of God." Nicodemus could not understand that a man could be born again when he is old.

Jesus explained it to him. "I tell you the truth, unless a man is born of water and the Spirit, he cannot enter the kingdom of God. Flesh gives birth to flesh, but the Spirit

gives birth to spirit. You should not be surprised at my saying, 'You must be born again'" (John 3:3, 5-7).

Three days later Karen was doing very well. Could she
possibly manage at home? Our home is like a spiritual nursery. Karen was a newborn baby in Christ. She had been placed
there as a newborn, requiring intensive care. Hers had been
a crucial birth and now she must be nourished with just the
proper formula and care until the critical stage was passed.
Now that she was stronger, it was time for the babe in Christ
to return to her home and family.

Arrangements were made for Paul to come for her. During our phone conversation, I spoke to him concerning his
own need for Christ. He appeared to be interested but wasn't
quite ready for a commitment. He thanked me for caring
and said he would be over soon to leave the girls and take
Karen home.

I met Paul and his two, beautiful little daughters at the
door. Before I showed him to the guestroom where his wife
was, I asked him if he had thought any more about accepting
Christ. He said he had been thinking about it a lot. He shifted
his weight, folded his arms and said, "I would like to know
what to do about it."

The door of opportunity was open, and I shared with him
how much God loved him. As I explained to him God's plan
of salvation, he listened carefully. He confessed Jesus as His
Lord, surrendering his life to Him. It was an emotional moment when we prayed, thanking God for the gift of His Son
and for helping Karen.

Karen was happy to see Paul. When he told her about his
decision in the living room, she threw her arms around him.
As they embraced each other, they shared their newfound
faith in Christ. Now that they were on the same team, they
could overcome anything, including the ridicule from Karen's

family, which was certain to come. They left the two girls with us until they were sure she was ready, which was only a couple of days. The family was back together, and a new life had begun for the four of them.

Paul and Karen were baptized and became faithful members of the church. The children completed the circle when, a year or two later, they made their decisions to follow Christ.

Although Karen's mother and other members of her family made it very difficult for her, she never gave up. After we moved from Indianapolis, we kept in touch. Later I saw Karen at a women's conference. Reflecting upon those early days of her new life in Christ, she smiled and said, "I praise God for the night I traded off my old life for a new life in Christ."

8
God with Us

It was Monday morning, March 11, 1991. The southern Indiana weatherman predicted a sunny, but cold day. A winter storm was brewing, but we did not expect freezing rain and snow until Tuesday. Merideth and I reasoned that we could get to Bunker Hill, which was north of Kokomo, Indiana, to pick up our new travel trailer and be home before the blizzard moved in.

We left early and arrived at Hal Dar's RV Sales by 10 A.M. The handicap modifications we had ordered for the trailer were done. Orientation of the functioning items on the trailer took so long to complete that it wasn't ready for us until late afternoon. The skies were dark, and winter was upon us. So we accepted an invitation to spend the night with some good friends in Bunker Hill.

Sounds of sleet and freezing rain woke us Tuesday morning. After breakfast, precipitation became light, and it seemed to be a good time to start home. It was only a short distance to the trailer. So far, so good. We backed up the van to hook onto the thirty-five-foot Dutchmen. Not so fast! The owner of the RV warned us of hazardous conditions, and advised us not to take our new trailer out on the highway. About that time we had noticed our van heater wasn't working. Rain had been freezing on our windshield, obstructing Merideth's vision. A new fuse was installed at the source of the trouble, and we retraced our tracks to Bunker Hill. The heater stopped again, but we made it into their drive safely.

Fortunately, our friends' neighbor was an experienced Ford mechanic. He tackled the job and corrected the complex problem. In the meantime, sleet, freezing rain and snow were on a rampage. It was obvious that we would not be venturing out and were destined to stay overnight.

The four of us decided to spend the evening playing table games. We were enjoying our little recreation when about 8:30 P.M. the electricity suddenly went off. All the lights went out, and since their home was all-electric, so did the furnace. The poor lighting from the candles was not enough to continue our games, so we prepared for a night's sleep. Our layers of activewear clothing would keep us warm. Never mind that we could hardly move under the blankets piled over us.

All was well until we woke up Wednesday morning to a chilled house. It was time to activate a distress call. The neighbors next door responded. Modes of transportation have changed through the years, but Merideth managed to get me through the deep snow via piggyback, placed me gently in a comfortable chair, and joined the men in search of more firewood.

We gathered around the living room fireplace, a welcoming backup system. An oil heater in the center of the kitchen not only kept the dining and cooking area warm, it also kept our coffee hot.

We were able to keep warm in layers of clothing. It was cold cereal for breakfast and tuna sandwiches for lunch. We ate to the sound of cracking flames from the fireplace and watched the sparks chase up the chimney. Merideth shoveled a path to the gas grill on their patio, and we had delicious hamburgers and hot dogs for supper. After eating by candlelight, we gathered around the dining table and played games. We were still wearing the same layered clothing that we put on the first night of the storm.

Bedding down for the night, we wondered if we would have electricity by morning. At two thirty Thursday morning, we awoke to lights all over the house and the furnace going full force. Someone got up and turned off the lights and returned to bed.

After a few more hours of sleep, covers were thrown back and one-by-one we awoke, shedding those layers of clothes. After breakfast the men plunged into the drifted snow with a snow blower and shovels. Back at our friends' home we enjoyed a good shower and hot lunch. Eating hot food was a blessing, for which we thanked our Heavenly Father. The bright sun warmed the earth, and snow and ice slowly became liquid.

Snowplows had managed to get both lanes of Highway 31 open by early afternoon. We checked on road conditions to see if we could start home. Although the ice storm was causing much chaos in that area, we were advised that, once we were past Kokomo, traveling would be fine. Our three-day winter vacation was about to end. We were informed by the owner of the RV Sales that they would bring our trailer out front to pick up about 3 P.M.

When Merideth backed up our van to connect the hitch to the trailer, we heard a shout from the man who was helping us. Our ball was too small. We must have a larger one

before we could hook up. This caused another delay. However, the new ball was installed, and we managed to get safely
on the highway before 5 P.M.

Great! We were finally on our way home. Or were we?
Once we were in our lane to start our journey home, we discovered that we had no trailer brakes. Very carefully, Merideth
drove until he found a place to turn around, which was north
of Kokomo. Once we were back on the RV Sales parking lot,
the problem was located and corrected. By this time it was
getting dark. At least everything was functioning and we were
soon back on the highway toward our home in Hope, Indiana. Finding a place to pull off and eat dinner was no problem, and before we knew it, Merideth was successfully backing
up that long, long, trailer into our drive about 9 P.M.

We praise the Lord and count our blessings each time we
reflect upon that ice storm. Each delay we experienced proved
to be a safety factor. An expert repaired the short in the ignition of the van and kindly waived the labor fee. The brake
problem was not new; we had been aggravated by it in the
past with our other trailer. An expert located it, fixed it, and
even showed us how to properly set our brakes.

We wonder how many major problems we avoided on
the highway because of those delays. Without a doubt, the
experience of being stranded in a devastating winter storm
turned our hearts to God, who protected us through it all.
Having just recovered from the flu, we were aware that God
had taken care of us and protected us from harmful exposure.
Psalm 32:7 came to mind: "You are my hiding place; you will
protect me from trouble and surround me with songs of deliverance."

God is our refuge and strength, an ever-present help in
trouble. Therefore we will not fear, though the earth give
way and the mountains fall into the heart of the sea,

though its waters roar and foam and the mountains quake with their surging. (Ps. 46:1-3)

God was our refuge in the ice storm, and He was there before a tragedy occurred. He protected and guided us and saw us safely home. We were stranded in an ice storm, but not without Him.

🍃 🍃 🍃 🍃 🍃

NEVER ALONE IN THE PARSONAGE

Being a shut-in is not all bad. Sometimes there are rewards in being alone, shut in from all the influences of the world. For example, when I looked through Christmas cards by myself, it was like sitting down for an intimate visit with friends and loved ones. I took advantage of a time to go down memory lane, imagining that person was sitting with me, face-to-face as I wrote to each one.

There are the quiet moments with the Word of the Lord. Alone? Never! God the Father, God the Son, and God the Holy Spirit are with me.

"If anyone loves me, he will obey my teaching. My Father will love him, and we will come to him and make our home with him" (John 14:23). Jesus promised us that we would never be alone.

Of the Holy Spirit, Jesus said to those who would believe in him:

And I will ask the Father, and he will give you another Counselor to be with you *forever* — the Spirit of truth. The world cannot accept him, because it neither sees him nor knows him. But you know him, for he lives *with* you and will be *in* you. I will not leave you as orphans, I will come to you. Before long, the world will not see me anymore, but you will see me. Because I live, you also will live. On that day (when the Holy Spirit comes in) you will realize that I am *in* my Father, and you are *in* me, and I am *in* you. (John 14:16-20)

My life is in Jesus. Jesus said in John 6:35, "I am the bread of life. He who comes to me will never go hungry, and he who believes in me will never be thirsty."

I am continually amazed at the truth of these words. Who am I that I should have the Son of God give me bread and water all day long? The parsonage is quiet when I am unable to be out on many winter days, but I never get thirsty or hungry, for He is with me. "His rod and His staff they comfort me . . . ."

If the clouds hide the sun and the parsonage becomes dark, I am reminded that I am never alone, and it is never really dark. Jesus is with me and light is all around. That's because He is light. For those moments when I become thoughtful of myself, the light of my Savior glows to remind me of His words, "I am the light of the world. Whoever follows me will never walk in darkness, but will have the light of life" (John 8:12b).

✿ ✿ ✿ ✿ ✿

Friends with Jesus

In preparing devotional thoughts for a Women's Fall Conference in 1986, John 15 spoke to my heart. I considered my spiritual growth with Christ. Did I understand what it meant to be promoted from a servant to a friend? First we are servants, knowing not what our master does. As we grow in Christ by abiding in His word and loving one another, we become His friend.

"You are my friends if you do what I command. I no longer call you servants, because a servant does not know his master's business. Instead, I have called you friends, for everything that I learned from my Father I have made known to you" (John 15:14-15).

I once lived by a couple who had a servant, a woman I'll call Mary. Mary came in each morning, always on time, to clean the house of this couple, whom I will call Mr. and Mrs. Ramsey. Mary also cooked and did whatever the couple requested. I was impressed with the relationship I saw between Mary and the Ramseys. They treated Mary with kindness, and Mary obeyed their instructions with respect.

Before Jesus talks of the relationship between friends, he clarifies the roll of a servant. He declares His love, and tells of His obedience to His Father.

> As the Father has loved me, so have I loved you. Now remain in my love. If you obey my commands, you will remain in my love, *just as I have obeyed my Father's commands* and remain in his love. I have told you this so that my joy may be in you and that your joy may be complete. My command is this: Love each other as I have loved you. (John 15:9-12)

Jesus speaks of experiencing joy when we obey the Father. We are still in the servant relationship with Him. The Ramseys did not share everything with their servant, Mary. And Mary knew nothing about their personal business. She only knew that the couple loved her and respected her, and she followed their instructions with joy.

Jesus said that when we move into a friendship with Him, then we are told everything about His Father. He keeps nothing from His friends. What a beautiful relationship!

"I have called you friends," He said, "for everything that I learned from my Father I have made known to you." As we grow in Christ by abiding in His word, and as we obey Him by loving one another, we become His friend.

Often we hear Christian speakers and teachers say, "I learn more in preparation than my hearers can possibly learn from my presentation." It is true: we learn by abiding in His Word. After all, we are His friends, aren't we?

9
Faith and Prayer

Summer goes, fall approaches. Winter comes and spring follows. Seasons come and go. In the spring, flowers break through their beds to remind us of the resurrection of our Lord. We celebrate Easter with songs of praise that "He is risen." We forget that the spring flowers withered and faded away when chilly winds and winter storms overwhelmed parts of the earth. Yet, all is not lost. They fell upon the soil, and as our Lord burst from the grave, the magnificent blossoms, green grass, and budding trees unfold. We are speechless at the beauty of the earth in the spring, all of which remind us of their Creator.

All life depends upon the Creator. According to His plan, it is important that seasons come and go. There is a time to plant, a time to prune, and a time to bring in the harvest of the fruit orchards. At the sight of the first bloom, we know fruit will follow. May God help me to plant seeds that will bring forth life and beauty in the lives of those around me.

It is easy for me to become selfish when I pray. Rather than spend all my prayer time expressing my desires for comfort and good health, I want to think of others, to love and to care for those around me. With all the physical ills, pain, and suffering, it is easy to concentrate on the need for physical healing. God has healed me many times, but I pray that He will not let me forget others who need His healing touch for their body and soul. I want to plant seeds that blossom from within.

Beauty and *fruit* from the soul of a person does not depend upon the four seasons; we can expect God's Word to bear fruit at any time. The salvation of souls and Christians bearing fruit are not restricted to seasons. Therefore, our prayers are never out of season.

In his prayer recorded in John 17:6-19, Jesus prayed for his disciples who were with him on earth. In verses 20-26, Jesus prayed for his followers and his church after them. People are constantly requesting that I pray for their lost loved ones, and they frequently request prayer for physical healing. Because of the special love I have for those who made the requests, I frequently return to John 17. I find strength from the example of Jesus' prayer for His loved ones. He made it plain that He was not praying for the world at this point, but for those of His who were in the world. I can almost hear Him call my name. Christ is praying for me when he says, ". . . those who believe in me through their (the original disciples) word, that they may all be one." Our prayers do make a difference.

$$\text{\textit{ll} \quad \textit{ll} \quad \textit{ll} \quad \textit{ll} \quad \textit{ll}}$$

GRANDMOTHER SPEAKS TO THE MOUNTAIN OF TEENAGE REBELLION

When our fourteen-year-old granddaughter came to visit us in the summer of 1983, she was confused, frustrated, and full of hate toward her stepmother. She would not trust her life to any adult. At the most critical time in her life she was faced with homelessness. This was my second time around with teenagers, and life with our daughters had taught me to call upon God for help when rebellion raised its ugly head.

Although Deanette had accepted Christ at the age of eight, it was her insecure family lifestyle that stunted her spiritual growth. To refuse her request to live with us and finish high school meant that she would become a ward of the court.

This lonely, rejected teenage girl was forced to make a painful transition in her life. With her chin touching her chest and her pouting lips thrust out in displeasure, she dared anyone to touch her. I knew she must be handled with tender, loving care. Through Deanette's childhood I had always helped her, but now I was confined to a wheelchair. Could I save her from a hopeless, sinking situation? How could I fit in? In spite of the risks, I had to say yes to her. The challenge was frightening.

Who would have believed that my disability would have proved to be the instrument through which Deanette would be delivered from her dilemma?

I was there for her. I began to absorb the emotional moods of each experience with her during the most crucial months of her life. The challenge was a mountain of teenage rebellion. Each day she isolated herself in her room. At times she refused to come out to eat. When there was an opportunity for dialogue between us, she dominated it with the onslaught of a terrified animal trapped in a cage.

Like melted rock issuing from a volcano, steamy, hot words shot out of her seething mouth. It was obvious that God had chosen me for the escape vent through which this infernal pressure could explode. Her body shook with sobs as she repeatedly fought for her identity. It was during one of those emotional episodes that I remembered the words of Jesus, instructing His followers about faith.

> Jesus replied, "I tell you the truth, if you have faith and do not doubt, not only can you do what was done to the fig tree, but also you can say to this mountain, 'Go, throw yourself into the sea,' and it will be done." (Matt. 21:21)

Was I dealing with a mountain? I read in *Vine's Expository Dictionary of New Testament Words* that a mountain is a natural raised part of the earth's surface, larger than a hill. Jesus speaks proverbially in Matthew 21:21 about overcoming difficulties and accomplishing great things. A mountain could be a financial burden, a physical problem, or any of life's difficulties.

No doubt about it, I was among the thousands of parents and grandparents who are faced each year with a mountain of teenage rebellion.

When I was forced to depend upon an electric wheelchair in 1981, I was devastated. As a pastor's wife and Christian leader, I was involved in numerous leadership activities. I had spoken to that physical mountain, which had interrupted my agility, and the stress was removed. However, such an obstacle was no match for the promontory which moved into the parsonage with Deanette. I must pray for the removal of this mountain.

One evening Deanette was out riding her bicycle with a friend. She promised to be back in time to assist me to the church for a meeting. When she was thirty minutes late, I called her grandfather at the church office for help. He began his search for her. In the meantime, our associate minister's wife had come to help me to the church. My husband's search for our granddaughter extended through the dark hours of the evening. He made a few telephone calls and drove throughout the town before he found her. Obviously, Deanette was not where she was supposed to be.

Her excuses were no surprise to me. "I forgot," she said, adding, "I thought you said 7:30 instead of 6:30."

When her friend, who was already in trouble with the law, was mentioned, Deanette said, "You think you have to pick my friends for me." Raising her voice, she shouted, "Why can't you believe me, just once? You always think I'm lying."

Her accusations hurled through the air, piercing my heart like a dagger. I reached into my storage bin of faith for strength and the right words. Right or wrong, I agreed with her about my lack of trust in her.

"That's right. At this point I can't trust you. You taught me not to trust you. Now you have to earn my trust." I hoped for a favorable reply.

"I'm sorry," seemed to be the magic words that would free her from my wrath. When I assured her that just saying she was sorry didn't work with me, her flippant response was, "Then what do you want me to say, Grandma?"

"Just tell the truth. That's all I ask. When you start being honest with me, you will be surprised how good the truth will make you feel." My voice softened a little.

Again, there was silence. She began to mellow, and in a moment of compassion I said, "What about it, honey? Do you want to try for the simple truth? Please help me trust you."

Her sudden reaction surprised me. With a thud she threw herself against me. Warm tears soaked my collar as she sobbed uncontrollably. She nestled her wet, warm face into the curve of my neck as I held her quivering body tightly against mine.

She saw I was weeping, too, and said, "Don't cry, Grandma, I will try. I promise. Will you help me?" Like warm butter, she melted in my arms.

"You bet I will. Shhh," I said, stroking her wet hair.

The vibration of the crumbling mountain of rebellion penetrated my body. I could hear its particles cracking to pave the way for communication between the two of us. Holy stillness followed, and her soft, sniffing sounds made background music for my prayer.

"Oh God, please make me an instrument of Thy peace, not a defensive grandmother."

The mountain was "cast into the sea." A miracle took place in our relationship, and Deanette gradually earned my trust.

Deanette used to proofread for me. As she finished reading this story, she said, "Grandma, I was a brat, wasn't I?"

"Yes, honey, you were," I agreed.

She raised her head and looked at me. "I was your mountain to speak to, big time, wasn't I?"

"Mmmmm, more like Satan's struggle to take you away from me was my mountain, not you," I corrected.

"I have really changed, haven't I Grandma?" She lightened up.

Smiling I said, "We sure have, sweetie, and from now on when a big-time problem rises up . . . ."

"I know," she interrupted.

With tears and laughter, together we said, "We'll speak to the mountain."

🌿 🌿 🌿 🌿 🌿

Walking by Faith, Not Sight

"How is it we walk by faith not by sight?" I wrote down soon after I was confined to the wheelchair. To place our faith in what we see may be deceiving. "We live by faith, not by sight," according to 2 Corinthians 5:7.

Mildred (not her real name), a young Christian wife and mother had prayed for her husband to trust the Lord. She saw God answer her prayers. Howard (not his real name) came to Christ a few months after Mildred was baptized and he was faithful to the church. Suddenly, his attendance slacked off. Howard had rejoined his beer-drinking friends. He was skipping church to stay home with them to watch sports.

What could we do to help? There were no magic answers for the moment. We must trust God for what we could not see. Matthew 18:19 says, "Again, I say unto you, That if two of you shall agree on earth as touching anything that they shall ask, it shall be done for them of my Father which is in heaven."

Repeatedly, I have claimed this promise with individuals praying for their loved ones. The results have been positive. God works miracles while we are not looking. Mildred needed a miracle. She was pleading for help as she wept over her husband.

"Mildred," I said to her. "I know one thing that works. Agreeing together as touching anything has worked often."

She listened as I shared with her some things that resulted as my husband and I claimed God's promises. We began claiming Matthew 18:19 early in our marriage, I told her, and through the years we have joined in prayer with others for their spouses. The promise that if "two of you shall agree on earth" about anything you ask for never fails.

Holding out my hand toward her, she placed her hands in mine. We prayed. Only the one who made that promise could meet her desire to have her husband back by her side in church. We asked God to touch Howard's heart and change his mind as we agreed together in prayer and promised to continue to pray until the answer came. Howard was not out of fellowship with God for long. God answered our prayer. After that, he remained faithful to God and his church.

Whether our desire is for a closer walk with God, a healing experience, or strength to carry a particular burden, we can find some person in whom we trust to agree with us in prayer on anything. Our answer doesn't depend upon our sight. If together we will claim God's promise to fill that need, He will do something for us. How long should we agree and pray? The answer is until we know that our request is answered.

In my prayer journal, I keep an account of each person for whom I have prayed. Recorded is the date upon which I began praying for a specific need, along with notes pertaining to that need. It is thrilling to pick up and check those special notes and see what God is doing. The date upon which we agreed with someone, the special needs, and the number of times we prayed together before the answer came, confirms that God is faithful to his promises.

Many of my friends and relatives prayed for my physical healing. Because of God's promise to hear us, we would not give up. I was dependent upon a wheelchair much of the time. My limited mobility was not because God was not listening.

I find great comfort in His presence and the strength for each day. I would continue to trust in Him for my every need. Jesus told Thomas, "Because you have seen me, you have believed; blessed are those who have not seen and yet have believed" (John 20:29). Jesus had much to say about seeking signs. Many want a sign. We walk by faith, not sight.

🍃 🍃 🍃 🍃 🍃

RECOGNIZING AN ANSWER

It was Sunday morning, October 15, 1989. The First Baptist 8:45 A.M. worship hour had just begun, and the choir was singing. Unable to control a persistent cough, I quietly eased my wheelchair down the aisle to make as graceful an exit as possible. Perry Harker met me outside to offer help. My independence told him I would be fine once I was out of the cool air. The Fortress scooter did her full six-miles-an-hour speed, while my coughing was nonstop. Once I got inside the parsonage, I was sure the coughing would cease.

But it didn't. In my living room I dropped to the big chair. I struggled for each breath and tried to control the cough. "Please, God," I prayed. "Either remove the stress or send someone to help me."

Before I finished asking God to help me, the phone rang. It was Perry calling to check on me. I admitted to him that I was having difficulty breathing, but I still did not wish to admit that I needed help. My independence surfaced, and I never wanted to impose upon anyone. Especially, I did not want to interrupt the worship that was in progress at church. Perry is a very compassionate person, and I knew he sensed that I was in trouble. As I was about to hang up he stopped me.

"Do you want me to send someone?" he asked.

Fear gripped me when I realized that I was about to let him go. Remembering that I had just asked God for help, I managed to say something.

"Yes, I do believe I need someone." I caught my breath as I stammered.

"OK," he spoke hurriedly, "I'll send someone right now."

Somewhat relieved, I let myself back into the big chair. Would I pass out before someone came? My body was growing weaker as I waited for help. Mae Jessee had come out of the choir to help me.

"What can I do?" she asked.

"Call the paramedics," I was out of breath.

I don't remember Mae making the call, but I heard the ambulance pull into the drive. Their voices were familiar as the men opened the storm door and rushed to my side. Charlie Biggs and Jerry Crouse, both volunteers, began to ask questions. Jon Dillman, a paramedic as well, was standing tall in front of me. Jerry, who was familiar with my problem, administered oxygen. Their voices faded away and the next thing I knew we were whizzing down the highway in the ambulance.

"Stay with me, Rae," Jerry kept saying as he applied the heart monitor and checked my vital signs. I heard him reporting to Charlie, who was sitting to my right, recording the readings. More alert by then, and in a sitting position, I could see through the back windows. Motor vehicles were pulled off the highway in response to the sound of the blasting siren and to swirling emergency signals. In no time I was in the emergency room. Ed Stone was adjusting the sheets as they carefully transferred me to a hospital cart. The hospital emergency team took over, with not a second lost in the transfer. After tests and treatment, I was released and returned to my home by early afternoon in our own handicap van.

As I continued to improve, I reflected back on that incident. I had prayed that God would remove the stress and send someone to help me. Within a breath, I almost turned away the very help I had asked for. I didn't recognize immediately that God was actually sending me help upon my request. How quickly He responded!

How often do we fail to recognize an answer to prayer when it comes. God had ways of taking care of me. My own neighbors, who are dedicated to saving lives, were ready to save my life upon God's call. After this incident, I grew in an understanding of how ready God is to respond to us, and how I should recognize an answer when it comes. Almost every day I find myself saying, "That is an answer to prayer. God heard me!"

10
Church (The Family of God)

ne body— many parts . . . ." Paul says the body is a unit. "Though it is made up of many parts; and though all its parts are many, they form one body" (1 Cor. 12:12).

A few years ago in Indianapolis, a human leg with the foot attached was discovered in Fall Creek. This body part was not simply tossed aside as a stick of dead wood. A detective squad went to work immediately to find the body to which it belonged.

When I was eleven, I was helping my Aunt Lula clean out the upstairs rooms of an old hotel across the street from where I lived. The building was being renovated so that my aunt and uncle could live there. Nothing is more fun for kids than going through discarded items; it is much like a treasure hunt. Our hearts pounded with excitement when one of our gang found a human thumb in an old pasteboard bin. It appeared to be a man's.

Our mystery solving juices began to flow. Where on earth did the human part come from? Was someone murdered in this old hotel? To whom did it belong? Like the body part that was found in Fall Creek, in our possession was this mysterious thumb from someone's hand. Our minds would not find peace until we found the answer. From one possible source around the neighborhood to another, we did our detective work. We questioned those who might be familiar with the old hotel and guests who had checked in through the years.

Alas! The mystery was solved. A neighbor told us of a medical student who had once lived in the hotel. What we had found was an object of her studies. Being children, it had never occurred to us that the body part had been treated with a preservative. Well, so much for that treasure. We tried to imagine how it would be for our hands to function without a thumb?

Each part of our body must function in harmony with other parts. So it is with members of a family. Other family members who are strong come to the aid of the weak. The weaker part is supported by stronger parts so that the family may function as one unit.

"Now the body is not made up of one part but many. If the foot should say, 'Because I am not a hand, I do not belong to the body,' it would not for that reason cease to be part of the body" (1 Cor. 12:14, 15). Paul was talking about the body of Christ, the spiritual body. God has arranged every part in the body, just as He wanted it. If the parts were all the same, where would the body be? Each part is necessary in order to function as a unit.

How often have we heard it said, "When my feet hurt, I hurt all over." That is true with any part of our body. If one part suffers, every part suffers, so that there should be no division in the body. The spiritual significance has been made graphically clear to me as I have coped with some weak body parts for more than thirteen years. I will continue, however, to receive special care and assistance from my loving husband, the stronger member of our family, until healing is completed. As the body of Christ needs the weaker parts of His body, so do I need the weaker part of my body. The peace I have is true assurance that I am a child of God, a part of the body of Christ. "One body, many parts" make up the whole.

✿ ✿ ✿ ✿ ✿

A Chosen People —— I Peter 2:9-10

"We are a chosen people, a royal priesthood, a household of God, a temple of the Spirit, a colony of heaven, and the body of Christ." The litany was shared between a speaker and a congregation in Cleveland, Ohio, in the summer of 1984. The national convention brought people from every state to take a look at our status with God.

"We are a chosen people" echoed in my heart long afterwards. "All Hail the Power of Jesus' Name" rang out as hundreds worshiped God.

I remember how that great auditorium expanded as the All Cleveland Mass Choir sang "Lift Up Your Heads O Ye Gates." For weeks my heart kept singing. My heart still bursts with praise as I consider the fact that I am a part of the colony of heaven and the body of Christ. I am chosen that I may declare the praises of Him who called me from darkness into His wonderful light.

God chose me long before I chose Him. I was nine years old when I invited Christ into my life, even before the minister finished his message. The minister said, "If you had been the only person in the world, Christ would have died for you, anyway."

In my childish mind I wondered how God could love me so much that He would give His only begotten Son for me. When I walked down the aisle alone that night, I made a lifetime commitment. Although my father suggested that I was too young and would not allow me to be baptized, nothing could change what happened that night.

Two years later I was baptized. Since I was eleven at the time, my Father was sure I knew what I was doing. God chose me to be a part of the colony of heaven and the body of Christ. He chose me to share His inheritance with His Son, Jesus. Why did God choose me? I Peter 2:9 tells me why: ". . . that you may declare the praises of him who called you out of darkness into his wonderful light." I never stop praising Him.

❦ ❦ ❦ ❦ ❦

Good News Class Success Story

When my husband became pastor of the First Baptist Church of Hope, Indiana, it was alive with new converts. That first year we were near the top among churches in the state for baptisms. Several teams were going out each Tuesday evening, presenting the plan of salvation to non-Christians.

The numerical growth caused a problem, but a good one. How could we invite young married couples to Sunday school when there was no class for them? They could join their parents or older adults in a class, or they could go into the postgraduate class. Something had to be done! Something was done. My husband and I took the matter to the board of Christian Education, which addressed the problem.

The church had just purchased a little house across the street from the main church building–a perfect place to begin a young adult department. We discovered many faithful young adults among our 650 members. They attended worship but not Sunday School. The field was white unto harvest. How could we interest them?

"Let's have a dinner—a kick-off dinner, " I suggested. We agreed to send out special invitations to every young adult, church member or not. The board appointed a committee and the idea carried through.

On the night of the dinner thirty-three young adults showed up. Two of our women staffed the nursery. There was no doubt about it. Good things were about to happen. Fellowship over dinner was cheerful. Enthusiasm mounted when the idea of classes was presented. Each one took a regular enrollment card, filled in the information, and enough people signed up to begin a new department with four classes. I was so sure it would work, I accepted the board's suggestion to head the new department and teach a Sunday school class.

With the French doors open between the living room and dining room of the little house, there was space for an opening exercise with singing, devotionals, and prayer before going to classrooms. Why not go directly into the classrooms? The answer was simple. The young adults would have an opportunity to get to know one another, and in a group setting, talents often are discovered and developed.

Our present music director, Howard Downey, is an example of such leadership development. Fresh out of Purdue University, he became our first department song leader. Many of our current teachers, trustees, and members of committees, including nine ordained deacons, are products of one of the new classes, the Good News Sunday School Class. Now, that is *making disciples*. The department started as scheduled.

The average attendance during the first month was twenty-five. The attendance report in the October newsletter read:

#1 Post-graduates   8
#2 ages to 25   10
#3 age 25-30   4
#4 age 30-35   2

The Good News Class began with less than a dozen. Organized in September, the class elected officers and appointed committees. Attendance ran from one to ten persons during the first few months. In January 1979 the enrollment was sixteen, fourteen active and two inactive students. Class meetings were set on the second Monday evening of each month, with a *pitch-in* meal. When the class grew too large for meeting in homes, the couples would host them in the fellowship hall. Babysitters were hired to care for the children during the class meetings that followed the meal. Sometimes as many as twenty-four children were present. In the meetings, class members learned organizational structure and proper business procedures that prepared them for leadership positions in the church.

Interest in evangelism grew. From the director of visitation, I secured cards with names of prospects for the class. Prayerful study was given for each family member listed, and class members chose the people whom they wished to visit. A telephone call was made to set up an appointment for a visit. The purpose of the initial visit was to get acquainted and invite them to Sunday school and morning worship. American Baptists call this "friendship evangelism." If complex question arose, a report was made to the director of visitation, who went with the member or members on the next visit.

Two things were accomplished by the second visit: (1) an experienced caller would clear up some questions the prospect had; and (2) class members learned steps of evangelism.

Out of the four classes in the department, the Good News Class and the postgraduate class survived. What happened to the other two? A class cannot survive when its teacher is inconsistent in attendance and preparation. Unfortunately that is what happened to those two classes.

In forty-three years of teaching and leadership in Sunday school, I have watched classes die because of a teacher's inability to teach a small class. If only one person showed up, I taught the lesson. A faithful teacher spends hours praying and studying with his or her students in mind. What a waste, if she or he fails to share it with even the one person.

What if just one person shows up? It happened once with a new Christian. His wife was ill. It was an excellent time for him to ask some crucial questions concerning his new life in Christ. I prayed with him over these concerns, and with the time left we discussed the lesson. That man is now one of our faithful deacons. Besides his faithfulness in his Sunday school class, he has been chairman of the church nominating committee and served on the board of trustees and other committees. How important it is for a teacher to count each class member important!

What if no one shows up? With the Good News Class that never happened. In the past it

"When no one showed up for her Bible class," Rachel said prior to her confinement to the wheelchair, "I prayed."

has. I would simply sit with my Bible and the record book on my lap and pray for each member. Is not absenteeism itself a call for prayer?

The Good News Class growth was on the rise. In the first three years, attendance went from eight to sixteen. By the fifth year, enrollment was thirty-eight; the average attendance was nineteen.

By the fourth year the class outgrew the space in the little house. A partition between two rooms in the church basement was removed. The class moved in, and continued growth brought in many children, creating a wonderful problem. The little house was converted into a children's building for ages two through preschool.

The Good News Class had reached its peak with an enrollment of forty-three. When a class becomes too crowded for space, growth slows down, stops, and the class starts to lose members. It is time to divide into two classes.

In the meantime, a muscle disease had made it painful for me to walk. As the disease progressed, the men of the class would help me down and back up the steps. When I was forced to use a wheelchair, the class switched rooms with a class on the main floor so I could continue to teach. Limited space was still a problem. In 1984 the Koinonia Crusaders class was begun. By April 1989 it had reached an enrollment of thirty-three, with an attendance of twenty-two to twenty-seven. The Good News Class had an enrollment of twenty-four, and averaged twenty-two to twenty-four.

In March 1989 my disability forced me to give up the Good News Sunday School Class. God had a faithful teacher ready. Both these classes would continue to grow. More children would fill our children's buildings, and through them the church would grow.

One Sunday in 1982, nineteen parents from the Good News Class presented fifteen children in a child-dedication service. These children were in our youth choirs and youth fellowship now.

Will this happen again? I think so. The Good News Class is sponsoring a new class for young, married couples this year. A couple from the class is committed to teach it. Our nursery and toddler rooms are crowded. A child dedication service is scheduled for Mother's Day, just the beginning of a new success story at First Baptist Church of Hope. How many leaders, teachers, and deacons will come from this class? That depends upon the faithfulness of teachers and "friendship evangelism."

Before the disease struck in the late 1970s, Rachel helped organize the Good News Class at her church.

Well done, good and faithful servant! You have been faithful with a few things; I will put you in charge of many things. Come and share your master's happiness! (Matt. 25:21)

First Baptist Church of Hope had had a problem in 1976, but not for long. There was a vision and it was fulfilled through a Sunday school class. Neil Jones, treasurer of International Ministries, ABC/USA, spoke in our church a few years ago. He inquired, "Where did all that young leadership come from?" Like Mr. Jones, many visitors ask the same question. I simply tell them "The Good News Class Success Story."

By 1984, the church's "friendship evangelism" campaign had created enough growth to begin a new "Koinonia Crusaders" class.

11
Daily Living

handbook comes with each piece of functional equipment we buy. The manual that came with my Fortress Scientific wheelchair explains the performance of my friend on wheels. It tells me of its safety features. The warnings are clear and precise. If I expect it to function properly, I must refer to the guidelines frequently. It must be ready to tackle any steep incline, or manage any rough terrain. The most important section in the handbook is the maintenance schedule. "Daily check the batteries," it reads. "Charge batteries with the battery charger provided with your unit." All other items under the schedule are to be checked weekly, monthly, and yearly.

The consequences for not following the checklist can be disconcerting and dangerous. It takes at least thirty minutes to fully charge the batteries. Sometimes I would tell myself that I have plenty of energy for my domestic chores. It is unlikely that I would need to go far from my home. I don't really want to stop long enough to charge up. Suddenly, the little indicator light on my switch box would start flashing. This little light told me I have a third of the battery's energy left. If I am wise, I will take the necessary time to bring it to a full charge.

I often panic when I think of the consequence of not being prepared for possible challenges. But the little light reminded me, *"Turn in, Rae. The batteries are getting weak. Caution! Stay on smooth surfaces—and DON'T PANIC! Just use the remaining energy with care."*

All this has a spiritual lesson for us. The Word of God is our source of energy for the believer. The Bible is our handbook for spiritual living. If we neglect reading it and following the instructions for daily living, we are taking risks. We may be too low on energy to meet the challenges of the day.

The opportunity to help a weak Christian, or to show a lost person how to be saved, may be our incline or our rough terrain over which we are too weak to travel. Our *indicator light* starts flashing. Perhaps we are unprepared to quote Scripture at an appropriate moment. We will not panic if we have daily checked the instructions in God's Word. We have no flashing light to worry about.

Here's a checklist for our daily maintenance, using the Holy Bible as our spiritual guide:

1. Avoid accidents. "You are in error because you do not know the Scriptures or the power of God, you are in error" (Matt. 22:29).
2. Take care. "Remain in me, and I will remain in you" (John 15:4).
3. Be careful! You are operating with full power! "For the word of God is living and active. Sharper than any double-edged sword, it penetrates even to divid-

ing soul and spirit, joints and marrow; it judges the thoughts and attitudes of the heart" (Heb. 4:12).

4. Read instructions carefully and memorize them for your protection. "Do not merely listen to the Word, and so deceive yourselves. Do what it says" (James 1:22).

5. "But the man who looks intently into the perfect law that gives freedom, and continues to do this, not forgetting what he has heard, but doing it—he will be blessed in what he does" (James 1:25).

6. Don't be afraid to operate on what you know. Share what you have with others. "I am not ashamed of the gospel, because it is the power of God for salvation of everyone who believes . . . : just as it is written: the righteous will live by faith" (Rom. 1:16,17).

7. If your indicator light flashes, it is a warning: You are weak—do not continue to operate in this weakened condition—go recharge with the Word of God. "My soul is weary with sorrow; strengthen me according to your word" (Ps. 119:28).

Just as I must keep the batteries charged daily for smooth operation of my Fortress, I must consult my spiritual handbook daily. I must be prepared to meet any spiritual challenge throughout the day.

ℓℓ ℓℓ ℓℓ ℓℓ ℓℓ

Ready or Not

We spent time in a recreational park on Highway 14 in 1994, making many trips to Palm Dale, California. In January our plans to return there were changed, so that we could be with our daughter and husband for two weeks in Las Vegas. On the last day of our fourteen-day stay in Las Vegas, we learned that our change in plans probably saved our lives. That is the morning a big earthquake hit. A policeman was killed on that highway to Palm Dale. The earthquake did considerable damage in the preserve where we had canceled out, and people were evacuated. We praised the Lord for His presence during that frightening time.

"But what if?" we may say. What if we had been on Highway 14 that early morning? These questions caused us to think. Ready or not, it could happen to us any time. It is necessary that we have our survival kit packed, so that we can survive physically if a quake or any other disaster strikes. What about our spiritual survival kit?

The most important preparation we can make is to be ready to face our God. If our physical survival kit is not fully equipped, we will physically suffer, but if we believe in God's Son, we will not perish.

> "For God so loved the world that he gave his one and only Son, that whoever believes in him shall not perish but have eternal life. For God did not send his Son into the world to condemn the world, but to save the world through him. Whoever believes in him is not condemned, but whoever does not believe stands condemned already because he has not believed in the name of God's one and only Son." (John 3:16-18)

Recently, I had a brother who was very ill. For several days he was on a life-support system. A heart attack left him "dead," as the doctor put it. The family had been called in to decide whether to disconnect the system. The heart pump was disconnected. The respirator was withdrawn. Unexpectedly, there was a heartbeat. Gradually the heart picked up its own beat. Leslie began breathing on his own, and the family knew they had a miracle. Within a few days he was home under loving care and doing well.

The significance about his recovery was that he was not ready to go. Yes, he was spiritually ready, but there were some unfinished physical preparations he needed to make with his wife, Helen, before his death. Not being ready, for Leslie, did not mean he was not a child of God.

Some, however, are spiritually unprepared. I ministered to a lady in Columbus, Indiana, who was on her deathbed. Rachel had accepted Christ, but she was having problems at the end. I was a patient in her room, and I knew her family. Her daughter and son-in-law were sitting beside her watching her die. It was at the close of the day when Rachel was mumbling something with an irritated voice.

"No," she said, "I don't want to go in there. Please, I will not go in there."

The daughter was frustrated, trying to talk to her. She was dying. I had been with many people during their last hours, but this struggle was frightening to her family. Slipping from my hospital bed, I asked the daughter to move back a minute and let me see if I could communicate with her.

Touching her hand, I called her name. "Rachel," I said softly. "What do you see?"

"It's heaven," said she. Angrily she murmured, "But I don't want to go in there with him."

"Who is in there?" I asked. "Whom do you see?"

"My ex-husband." She called his name and continued. "I hate him. I don't want to go as long as he is there."

As Rachel's roommate, I had learned that her ex-husband was in the waiting room all the time she was there, but she wouldn't let him come in to see her. Their relationship had not been a pleasant one, and she didn't want him around.

Aware of this information, and knowing how painful an unforgiving spirit was, I was able to lead her to forgive him. When she understood the forgiveness of Christ, she said she would forgive him.

"Are you ready to go in to Jesus, now?" I asked.

"Yes," she drawled, "I am ready to go in."

Rachel was ready to meet Jesus, but she had that one thing to settle. She needed to forgive her ex-husband.

Rachel didn't die that night. We had been praying that she could go home to be with her daughter and grandchildren. Before she died, she had two months in her home to enjoy her grandchildren and family. Her brother, who was a member of our church, said she died in peace. Forgiveness brings peace, and God forgives us when we forgive.

People do not always have the chance that Rachel and my brother had. Our future lies with God. "I consider that our present sufferings are not worth comparing with the glory that will be revealed in us" (Rom. 8:18).

ℓℓ ℓℓ ℓℓ ℓℓ ℓℓ

Packing for a Trip

It was June 15, 1989. The place was Hope, Indiana. Early in the morning Merideth and I were preparing to leave for a national convention in Milwaukee, Wisconsin. Since we would be towing a travel trailer, I packed with care.

While checking my list, the image of Noah and the ark came to mind. Noah had an awesome responsibility to fulfill the specific instructions for loading the ark. I imagined what it would be like to load our trailer, knowing that as soon as we pulled out of the drive, a flood would destroy everything we left behind. What would I take if I knew we could never return? What would I leave behind? There was nobody to make that decision for me. Noah had to make sure he followed God's instructions very carefully, because the future depended on his obedience. The propagation of the animal kingdom depended on strict obedience. The future of God's people depended on his obedience. The birth of Christ depended on his faith.

My list was long. Many of the items on it would never be used, but I packed them anyway. Pausing to consider each item in hand, I convinced myself that I was being wise to include it. Obviously, I had much to learn about RV traveling, but packing everything on my list was the most convenient way for the physically challenged. With the inclusion of each article, I rationalized, "If I do need it, then I'll have it."

Once we were parked on a site, the burden of handling luggage and finding a place each morning to eat breakfast was eliminated. This is especially important for a physically challenged person. Not only is it risky to cross streets in the middle of a block, but often by the time we find a restaurant equipped for wheelchairs, we're both starved and running late.

I wonder how long it took Noah to decide how much food to take for each animal. How much for his family? I wonder if Noah discovered he had forgotten something? Do you suppose his wife took inventory after it was too late? The future depended on him. The flood was coming. Every person on the earth would be destroyed. Only Noah's family and all the animals on the ark would be spared. Accuracy was imperative.

There was a great difference between Noah's packing and mine. My responsibility was to decide what I needed for two people that would last two weeks. There was time to make decisions and then change my mind. Noah had no time to spend in confusion and indecision. Being a man of faith, he was obedient to all that God required of him. In spite of those who made fun of him, he never wavered. Unlike Noah, my preparation for a trip does not depend upon a definite weather warning. A predicted flood that would destroy the entire earth did not concern me. My packing was temporary. After a couple of weeks, we would return home, unpack and everything would be as before the trip.

Let There Be Light

A couple of men from the church had been working for several hours installing a new light in the parsonage study. As I flipped the switch, I said, "Let there be light!" and light flooded the room.

What that light did for my office reminded me of the Holy Spirit's work. I had worked with insufficient lighting for a long time. The new lighting revealed many things. It was easy to see that I had forgotten the office inventory. The best I could remember was the monitor and the display lights on the front panel. Those little red and green lights on my equipment told me what was working and how it was working. After the printer stopped, I would rip the hard copies off and take them to a window, or a better light, to read them.

It was the cobwebs, dust, and clutter in the office that attracted my attention once the light was on. Some things I had lost jumped out at me. My filing, which I thought was current, was waiting in a pile to challenge me.

Well, what did I do? I went to work. Steadily, and with a great deal of persistence, I kept responding to what the light revealed. I cleaned the cobwebs and put things back in order. Later, I noticed that Merideth had declared war on the surface dust. With the flip of a switch, there was light and new revelations! The mystery of many hidden items was revealed.

I felt a little like Paul must have felt when the light of Christ blinded him. Only for Paul, it took a little longer for his sight to return. Within a few seconds my eyes were adjusted to the sudden change. Jesus said this about the Holy Spirit:

> When he comes, he will convict the world of guilt in regard to sin and righteousness and judgment; in regard to sin, because men do not believe in me: in regard to righteousness, because I am going to the Father, where you can see me no longer; and in regard to judgment, because the prince of this world now stands condemned. (John 16:8-11)

First, the Holy Spirit convicts us that we are sinners. We respond and trust in Jesus, at which time the Holy Spirit comes in to dwell within us. Like a powerful spotlight, He focuses upon every piece of clutter and cobweb of our lives. We see these sins in our lives, confess them, and become new people. Because of the working of the Holy Spirit, we become new.

12
Miracles and Blessings

Kenny, my great-nephew, was four. His battle with a brain tumor, medulloblastoma, continued. Everything possible was being done. Surgery was unsuccessful. After eight days, a shunt was installed to allow fluid to drain into his stomach. Merideth and I were scheduled for a trip to Wisconsin, but first we stopped by the Methodist Hospital in Indianapolis to see Kenny.

It was the day after Kenny's surgery when we entered his room. A very sick little boy fixed his glassy eyes upon us. He seemed to know who we were, but his pale face gave no expressive reaction. He only stared at us and gave a grunting sound. Kenny and I had bonded before he was diagnosed with cancer, and even more so afterwards. However, I was never quite sure if it was me, or the scooter, that attracted him. His lack of response that afternoon indicated that he wasn't interested in either.

As I transferred from the wheelchair into a rocking chair beside his bed, his grandmother said, "He hasn't spoken since surgery. All we can get from him are peculiar sounds. We thought maybe you could get him to respond."

"I don't know" I replied. "Can he hear?"

"He seems to hear. He just can't speak words to let us know what he's thinking." Grandmother looked tired and weary as she spoke.

"Hello, Kenny. Do you know me?" I asked, as I waited for a response.

He tried very hard to respond, but only screeching sounds revealed his frustration. Kathy, his mother, was having very little success, but she was working with him patiently. The few words he attempted were accompanied by stressful struggles and high-pitched cries.

After we were certain that he had recognized me, I spoke to him again. "Kenny, do you remember when I went on vacation to Disney World?" I waited for a sign that he understood me, and added, "You asked me to send you a card with the picture of a lion on it? Remember that? But you did get a card from me, didn't you?"

After a little noise from him, I knew he could understand what I was saying, so I went on. "Remember? I couldn't find a card with a lion on it, so I sent you one with a bear on it?"

From that question there came a weak nod of his head. Thrilled that he was communicating, I continued. "Well, I am going on a vacation very soon. I will send you another card, OK?"

Another weak nod showed us that he was on track. We watched and listened anxiously for anything from him.

"What would you like on the card this time, Kenny? Can you tell me?"

"BEAR!" He blurted out the word loud and clear. Neither his face nor his eyes revealed expression.

"Praise the Lord!" his grandmother cried.

"Praise the Lord!" I echoed. With an effort to control my emotions, I continued as quietly and calmly as possible. "Well then, if I send you two cards, what picture do you want the second one to have on it?"

"LION," he responded with less effort.

"All right!" I shot back. "I will try my best, and if I can't find a bear or lion, I'll pick a card I think you will like. OK?"

He nodded his head affirmatively.

Chuckles of joy filled his room. Getting my emotions under control, I said, "Well Kenny, is there anything else you would like for me to bring you?"

He nodded his head, indicating he had something in mind. So I asked, "What do you want?"

"Ice cream." Frustration had left his voice and he spoke more naturally.

Now I was frustrated. "Well, Kenny," I said with a chuckle, "I'm afraid ice cream would melt before I get back from my trip. How about if I get you some ice cream right now?"

With gestures he told me that he would like some ice cream momentarily.

"You got it!" I said, as I left the room with Merideth. "We'll be right back."

We returned with the ice cream and were thrilled at his response. With his unsteady arms Kenny reached for the ice cream. Like a little puppy he lapped up his treat. He ate as quickly as his grandmother could spoon-feed it to him. The slurping sound faded away as we left his room and walked down the hall. God had worked another miracle in Kenny's life. Exiting the hospital, Merideth and I felt good about our visit with Kenny.

"Kenny's battle against 'the bad guy' cells is ahead, isn't it?" I said to Merideth.

"You bet," he responded.

A little booklet, *Talking With Your Child About Cancer*, was written to help children understand their illness.

> Simple explanations about his illness are also important. Stories that relate the concept of cancer to ideas the child is familiar with are helpful in explaining the diagnosis; these comparisons may be tailored to the child's specific cancer type. The 2-to 7-year-old, for example, has some concept of good and bad and may understand his disease in terms of a battle between 'good guy cells' and 'bad guy cells'; taking his medicine will help the good guys become stronger so they can beat the bad guys.[1]

Kenny understood what was happening to him. His battle between the "good guy cells" and the "bad guy cells" ended when he was twelve. He lived a good, faithful life, handling his disease well. He touched the lives of all who knew him. Before he went home to his "Wonderful Savior," as he put it, he arranged his own funeral.

But before his death, each member of his musical family sang their best at the hospital in a tribute to Kenny. His room was filled with his favorite lyrics while he was transferring from his earthly life to his eternal home. His three aunts and his mother harmonized his favorite hymns. His Pa Pa Daddy (the grandfather who helped raise him) sang, "It Is Finished." When he ended with the line, "and Jesus is Lord," Kenny was almost gone. With his weak voice, Kenny said, "I like that song."

It was a difficult for him, but because of Kenny's special request, Pa Pa sang "It Is Finished" at Kenny's funeral. At the

---

1 "Talking With Your Child About Cancer," U.S. Department of Health and Human Services, Bethesda, Maryland, p. 5

foot of the casket, Pa Pa belted out the final words, "and Jesus is Lord!" The atmosphere was swollen with the power of the Holy Spirit; there was not a dry eye in the sanctuary.

None of us wanted to lose Kenny; neither were we selfish enough to want to keep him in his suffering. He deserved better. His physical death did not nullify the miracles that took place because of Kenny's life. When he said "BEAR" and "LION" that afternoon in his hospital room, it was a miracle. Each time the cancer was arrested, it was a miracle. Testimonies of new converts tell of their miracle because of Kenny's witness, but the greatest relief for Kenny was when his "Savior" called him home.

🍃 🍃 🍃 🍃 🍃

God's Extras

From where I sat in the wheelchair one cool morning, I noticed some little *extras* from our Creator. Isn't God good? He dresses up our lawns with colorful tulips and daffodils. The flowers could have been black-and-white, but God chose to dazzle us with colors. I heard a man speak on God's bonuses once. He mentioned the special bonus of colors and how black-and-white television viewing was enhanced by color.

The robins were building their nests. A pair of cardinals showed off their red beauty.

I marveled at the robins as they prepared for their little family. For nearly a week I had been watching this little female busily building her nest. She only stopped long enough to feed herself. On the run, she carefully builds her nest with bits and pieces of grass and twigs. If all human beings would make such careful preparation for their offspring, children would have a much better chance of survival. I thank God for his extras, as Margaret K. Frazer, a famous poet, says it so well in this poem:

God could have made the sun to rise
Without such splendor in the skies;
He could have made the sun to set
Without a glory greater yet.

He could have made the corn to grow
Without the sunny, golden glow;
The fruit without those colors bright,
So pleasant to the taste and sight.

He could have made the ocean roll
Without such music for the soul—
The mighty anthem, loud and strong—
And birds without their clear, sweet song.

The God who fashioned flow'rs and trees,
Delights to give us things that please,
And all His handiwork so fair
His glory and His love declare.

Yes, He who made the earth and skies
Gave *extras* for our ears and eyes,
And while my heart with rapture sings.
I thank Him for the "extra things."

Deliverance: God's Time or Mine?

Because Paul had freed a slave girl from an evil spirit, he and Silas were thrown in jail (Acts 16:16-34). What an undignified, humiliating position for two of God's servants!

"Surely God will deliver them from a night in jail, because this makes Christ look bad," some would reason today.

Picture this. A group of gifted Christians rallying around the jail for the release of these two men of God, believing that God did not want His children to spend a night in jail. Lifting signs high in the air, they shout their pleas in the name of God. Can you hear them calling upon the two men to have faith for an instant miracle of deliverance?

While Paul and Silas did pray, there is no account that they prayed for themselves. The two men were put in an inner cell and their feet were fastened in stocks. That's degrading as well as uncomfortable! The worst part about it was that they were treated "as other prisoners." That would really disturb us today, wouldn't it? But those "crazy" men, rather than cry out, "Deliver us!" prayed and sang hymns at midnight (Acts 16:25). And, don't forget, these men had been stoned and flogged, so that they were also in need of a physical healing.

The Scripture says that "the other prisoners were listening." While we are trying to diagnose a situation on the outside, let's not forget something more important might be happening on the inside. These "weird" men were singing and praying in all their pain and suffering. They weren't even following a special outlined plan of salvation. In fact, it appears that they were not aware of the other prisoners. They were just praising God!

Suddenly, there was a great earthquake that shook the foundations of the prison. The doors flew open. Everybody's chains came loose. The jailer woke up seeing the doors open. Frightened, he drew his sword to kill himself because he thought the prisoners had escaped.

Paul shouted, "Don't harm yourself! We are all here!"

The jailer called for the lights, rushed and fell trembling at the feet of Paul and Silas. Bringing them out, he asked, "Sirs, what must I do to be saved?"

Don't we know that the jailer and his household are forever grateful that no one bailed those two men out of prison? What a night to remember and for which to praise the Lord! If nobody ever suffered, then none of us would be saved. Of course, the ultimate suffering was the death of Jesus on the cross.

It is so important for us to pray "in God's will." Paul and Silas were on their way to "the place of prayer" when all this started. I don't think God enjoyed the men's suffering, but because of their faith in God, they were praising Him.

The scripture doesn't specifically say what they were praying for in the jail, but I discover daily that there are many people for whom I can pray; not just for me, mine, and ours.

I pray for opportunities from where I sit to respond to someone's cry, "Rae, what must I do to be saved?" Or perhaps someone with a need may call on the phone seeking help. May God help me not to be so engrossed in myself that I do not recognize such opportunities.

There are times when God heals instantly, and there are other times when he takes His time. Those of us who wait for physical healing must never give up; neither should we be frustrated because He doesn't do it "right now." In the meantime, my heart will go on singing with joy because of the faithfulness of God. I've had a miracle of instant healing. I've had a miracle of gradual healing. There were times when God did not follow my specific blueprint for a situation. His time is best and He is always and forever worthy to be praised.

ℓ℮ ℓ℮ ℓ℮ ℓ℮ ℓ℮

The Wristwatch Finds an Expert Repairman

A few years ago, I made up my mind I was going to have a little gold watch repaired. Our daughter, Katy, gave a matching set of heart-shaped, gold watches to Merideth and me on our 25th wedding anniversary. Mine had stopped and was put away sixteen years ago.

When I took the treasure to a popular jewelry store in Columbus and handed it to a clerk, she quoted from her repair-and-cleaning chart a fee of fifty dollars. While she was checking it out, she dropped the tiny crown on the floor, dropped to her knees and scanned the floor for it. At this point, I decided not to pay the fifty dollars and forget the crown. Just as I turned to leave, she came up with it. I took it, thanked her, and left.

Across the street, at the corner jewelry store, I handed the watch to the clerk, telling her what I thought was wrong with it.

"How much would your repairman charge for cleaning and repairing this watch?" I asked.

"Well, he's not working this week, but I'll take it back and ask someone about it," she replied.

She was only gone a few minutes. "Here, it should be OK now. The man tightened it and wound it, and it seems to be working," she said, handing it to me. "Check it out," she added. "If it doesn't work, bring it back. Cleaning and repair should run no more than thirty dollars."

Surprised at the fast service, I said, "Great, how much do I owe you?"

"Nothing," she answered with a smile.

"Thank you so much!" I said as I turned to leave.

It all happened so fast that I was somewhat doubtful about how well it would continue to run. I was sure I would be back for a cleaning job. All the way home I noticed it would tick a few seconds, then stop. Each time I would reset it, shake it gently until it started again, and it would run a few seconds longer; first a few seconds, and then minutes. By the time I was home, it had run at least ten minutes. I felt hopeful that it would continue to run. It had been wound too tightly and it just needed to be helped along to loosen up.

The watch was working well when I went to bed that night. The next morning I noticed that it had run several hours before stopping. In a couple days it was keeping perfect time and was as good as new. My favorite, little gold watch was running again, and it had not cost a penny. It had only taken a touch of an expert's hand to make it like new.

As I pondered this experience, it took on a whole new meaning about how God's children respond to brokenness.

Often we become ineffective. We malfunction or stop all together. A small obstacle begins to slow us down. We step back, face forward, and make our way through the barrier. Just when one obstacle is conquered, another comes. We become weak and tired, but somehow we get going again. Like my watch, we stop short, and it seems we will never go again.

Finally, completely run down, discouraged with life, we turn to a friend, a relative, or perhaps our minister. We may become completely run down, or as the watch, we may get wound too tight. After running in circles, we take a look at ourselves and realize that there are so many things wrong we can scarcely remember the initial problem. Friends and relatives offer help. They fail. The minister listens and offers spiritual counsel. Still nothing. Professional counselors are too expensive.

Finally, after all else has failed, we turn to God. In the same way that I turned the watch over to the expert repairman, we must turn our broken lives over to the expert repairman.

God takes one look at our problem and, with one touch, hands it back to us. "It's all right now. Go with it, and if it doesn't work properly, bring it back." Since He is our Creator, He knows exactly what makes us tick.

How costly it becomes for us to run here and there with our brokenness when one touch of God can repair anything that goes wrong. That's when we discover that what we had thought was wrong about us, wasn't it at all. It was just one little part that renders us spiritually ineffective and unproductive.

When I look at this little watch and see how it is keeping time, I can't help but reflect upon the repairman who fixed it. When I see myself enjoying God's presence after difficulties, I can't help but reflect upon the one who touched the wrong and made it right. And He does it for free. After all, He created us. Who knows best how to fix what is wrong with us?

"God is our refuge and strength, an ever-present help in trouble" (Ps. 46:1).

13

Delivered From A Wheelchair After Fifteen Years

Since the article, "From Where I Sit," in the first chapter of this book, was published, I never gave up the vision of being healed from the muscular dystrophy diseases.

First, there was polymyalgia rheumatica, an infectious attack upon the muscle caps and tissues. It weakens the body, making it vulnerable to polymyositis, a neuromuscular disease causing a weakness of neck and limb muscles, and is sometimes associated with malignancy.

Polymyositis did not surface in my body until 1993, from which time (*doctors said*) the two neuromuscular diseases could only be controlled, not cured.

The addition of another disease did not discourage my faith that I would be delivered from the wheelchair in His time. I never felt that my condition was permanent. The fact that Jesus Christ lives in me, He in the Father, and I in Him, was my hope to be well again. When there was doubt, He gave me faith. When I was weak, He made me strong, and when my impatience flared, He reminded me of His promises in chapter fourteen of John's Gospel.

> Don't you believe that I am in the Father, and that the Father is in me? The words I say to you are not just my own. Rather, it is the Father, living in me, who is doing his work. Believe me when I say that I am in the Father and the Father is in me; or at least believe on the evidence of the miracles themselves. I tell you the truth, anyone who has faith in me will do what I have been doing. He will do even greater things than these, because I am going to the Father. And I will do whatever you ask in my name, so that the Son may bring glory to the Father. You may ask me for anything in my name, and I will do it.
>
> If you love me, you will obey what I command. And I will ask the Father, and he will give you another Counselor to be with you forever—the Spirit of truth. The world cannot accept him, because it neither sees him nor knows him. But you know him, for he lives with you and will be in you. I will not leave you as orphans; I will come to you. Before long, the world will not see me anymore, but you will see me. Because I live, you also will live. On that day you will realize that I am in my Father, and you are in me, and I am in you. (John 14:10-20)

It was through an intense study of these promises that my husband, Merideth, and I renewed our faith in answered prayer for healing. In the first year of our marriage, daily miracles had manifested themselves as we poured over the Scriptures. Now, at age seventy two, fifty two years later, I have learned that Jesus is still the same. Nothing is impossible with Him.

Like two small children, we went to our Father, asking Him to heal hurts, illnesses, and various diseases that were causing a slow death in our small church family. As we concentrated on their needs, we included prayer for my healing. Results can best be told from a published story of my healing. This little sixteen-page booklet has been read by hundreds of people who have shared how God has blessed them through it. The following is the original text of that booklet.

✿ ✿ ✿ ✿ ✿

Part One: Written September 11, 1997

In 1979 I was diagnosed with polymyalgia rheumatica, a neuromuscular disease. However, the most challenging weeks with this painful disease came in August of 1997.

My husband and I were engaged in an intense search of the Scriptures. With our little church in mind, we poured over God's promises in His Word to find healing, healing for our church and for ourselves. We needed a revival in the church if she would survive. It wasn't such a big deal when I was in the wheelchair. I had found a way to serve and live for Christ from where I sat. I never gave up that I would be healed and delivered from the wheelchair someday. Thus I lived each day doing the best I could for Jesus' sake. There was always a way to serve the Lord with my writing, continuing with my activities with my husband, and just knowing that Jesus was in me; He was in His Father, and I was in Him.

October 1996 I visited the Muscular Dystrophy Association Clinic for an annual evaluation. No longer able to operate either of my scooter wheelchairs, the MDA neurologist, Dr. Robert Gardner, prescribed a custom power wheelchair for me. It was operated by a joystick with my right hand. When the chair was ready for me, I noticed the cost of $4,000, and I was troubled. Even with the help of insurance and the MDA, the cost was so much.

I had the feeling in my spirit that I would not need it very long. However, my caretakers went full speed ahead to make me comfortable. When you are one of Jerry Lewis' kids and God's kid at the same time, what else can you hope for?

I needed a divine miracle. It was Tuesday before Labor Day in 1997 when I went to the doctor. My comfort level had dropped to the bottom. I could not use my fingers. My arms would not work without severe pain; my neck and shoulders wreaked with pain. My feet and legs were swollen. It was the worst week of approximately twenty years with muscular dystrophy, and an accompanying acute arthritis.

I was told that the doses of medications were at the maximum. The doctors sorrowfully announced that they had done all they could do for me. With a discouraged heart, I tucked a prescription in my purse and went home feeling almost hopeless. Throughout the week I prayed for relief as I tried to renew my faith in a miracle.

Getting ready for church the following Sunday morning was a challenge. However, worshiping with my church family, and hearing the Word of God, was very important to me. Seldom did I miss church in the fifteen years I was in the wheelchair. As I sat thinking on Jesus and how good He was to me, even in the chair, I scanned the small congregation. My heart was disturbed as I prayed for each one and for a healing for our entire church. My own healing became less important. However, I thought of how much more I could help Merideth if I were made whole. If I could be healed, then I could, in turn, give them more hope.

The time came to go to the evening worship. With my elevated leg-rests attached to my wheelchair I was able to tolerate the hour.

On my way home from church I stopped to chat with a neighbor who was out watering her plants. My neighbor and I discussed a couple of *terminally ill* people in her family. We talked of claiming God's promises for healing, and I expressed my faith to her that I would be delivered from the wheelchair. I excused myself and started home, which was two doors down the street.

"I just know I am going to get out of this wheelchair some day," echoed in my spirit.

But as I rolled down the sidewalk, I was troubled. Did I really believe God was going to answer my prayers as He promised? Once inside the parsonage, I transferred my painful body over to my recliner. My spirit was broken, and I wondered why it was taking so long for God to answer our prayers for my healing.

Normally, I watch the Jerry Lewis Muscular Dystrophy Telethon on Labor Day weekend, but my troubled spirit caused me to flip through the channels.

"The reason why some people cannot receive healing is this." The words caught my attention, and I stopped flipping the button. A minister was discussing prayer and finding healing for any captivity. He mentioned healing of the physical body, marital problems, financial problems, and many things that kept us in bondage.

When you are on a diet, or trying to reform a bad habit, did you ever notice how alert you are to hear any words that relate to that subject? A voice telling you that someone has found a solution to your problem gets your attention, doesn't it? Because you are searching for a solution, you catch every word you can.

The same thing is true when one is on a spiritual quest. While I was searching for a spiritual solution through the Word of God, I was open for any help I could get from anyone.

The words I heard related to my need. With my present suffering and pain, and my search for healing for the church and my disease, I held onto every word.

"Here is why most of us cannot find our healing, be it for marital problems, financial difficulties, or physical healing." The minister went on to say that you can't mix the spiritual with the carnal. "We say, 'I believe in healing, but. I believe God answers prayer, but.'"

He said that when you mix the spiritual with the carnal, and your focus is on the healing, your pain and discomfort, then you end up with a god. That god is you. You are so involved with the desire to be healed that you cannot go beyond the healing to the healer. Focused on the healing, our body becomes our god. Focus on the healer, then the Lord Jesus is our God, and healing can happen.

"He's speaking about me," I said to myself. *"Surely, I have been so anxious to be healed that I have not seen beyond that healing for some time."*

As he spoke God's Words and discussed His faithfulness to keep His promises for us, I knew it was for me. He dared to ask the question, "Do you believe God will do what He says, or not? Do you believe that He hears you?" Questions like, "Why are you praying in the first place?"

That, too, made sense to me. If I don't believe the Word, and if I can't ask anything in Jesus' name expecting him to do it, then why do I read the Word? Why not toss it aside, forget His church and all that it stands for.

But I do believe the Word. I do believe that if I abide in Him and He abides in me, I can ask anything in His name and He will give it to me.

When the speaker said that faith and doubt do not mix, I knew God was speaking to me. The past few weeks I had been focusing my attention upon my healing rather than Jesus, the healer. I knew I must see beyond my pain and comfort level and refocus. I must look beyond the man who was speaking the Words of God for my hearing, look beyond my pain and suffering. I asked the Holy Spirit for help. I wanted to see Jesus, the healer, again.

After this God-sent message, the messenger invited his listening audience to rekindle faith in God for their needs, to cry out to Jesus in simplicity and not give up. I did.

"Lord, Jesus, I do give you everything I have. I give you my durable equipment (three wheelchairs, a walker on wheels, shower and bath stools, quad cane, cuff crutches, and many others)." I turned them all over to Him.

I gave Him this book. My condition had caused me to worry whether I would be well enough to get it to the publisher. I told Him that He could have it. If I never got it published, it would be OK. I gave Him my broken spirit, my body overcome with pain, and I finally said, "Lord, I surrender all I have. Please heal me!"

I sat back in my chair for a few minutes, looked over at Merideth, who was quietly praying with me, and said, "It's up to Him now."

Nothing spectacular happened, except a soothing peace flooded my body and soul. There was no electrical current or high energy of emotion, but I knew the struggle was over.

I got up from the chair and walked a few steps, turned around, and walked back to the chair. Walking the few steps was no big deal. I have done it many times, though later I realized that this time there had been no pain in the steps.

Not getting too excited, and knowing it was bedtime, I arose and walked through the hall. Later, I realized I had not held onto the walls, and there had been no pain.

Still not too excited, and not sure just what had happened, I sat in the wheelchair and moved it to the office, which is next door to my bedroom. Normally, I park the chair beside my bed to use it during the night.

I stepped into the bedroom and started to turn the cover down. When I took hold of the cover and pulled it up slightly, I noticed there was no pain. For the past few weeks I couldn't even handle the covers.

"Pain's gone," I said to Merideth.

"Good," he replied, "That's great."

I went to bed and experienced the most peaceful night's rest I've had in years. Like a tiny baby cradled in the arms of Jesus, I slept peacefully. He seemed to be saying, *"It's OK now. Go to sleep and rest."*

When I awoke on Monday morning, Labor Day, the first thing I wanted to do was check my hands. I moved them. They didn't hurt. I said to Merideth, "No pain in my hands this morning."

"Great, that's great!" His enthusiasm had picked up a little steam.

"Well, Lord, let's check out the rest of me," I said, swinging my legs out one at a time and placing my feet on the floor. I became more excited.

"No pain, Merideth," I said.

His reaction became more enthusiastic when he said, "Great. That is great."

That Labor Day morning my feet touched the floor, and I never stopped running. I was like a toddler, just learning to walk. My legs were somewhat like sponge, but I couldn't stop myself from walking. I haven't been in the wheelchair since.

Our church family was excited. I couldn't thank them enough for their prayers for my healing. I wanted to recognize the prayers of friends and loved ones throughout the world who have been praying for me, many of them for nearly twenty years.

God does hear the prayers of the saints. A priority on my list in telling what God has done for me is to thank all who have prayed for me through the years. We've been to Indiana to thank family members and members of churches, where we have served. We want to show them what God has done, that He is real and alive. The celebrations have been such a blessing.

✿ ✿ ✿ ✿ ✿

PART TWO: WRITTEN NOVEMBER 14, 1997

Wednesday was a day we were excited about. I went to the Muscular Dystrophy Clinic in Cape Girardeau, Missouri, for my annual evaluation. My local doctor had prepared a report and copies of my blood work to take with me.

It was an exciting day. The receptionist was ecstatic when she saw me walk into the waiting room. There was hugging and a little weeping. The therapist, Tina, who always took care of me, was more shocked than anything. She introduced me to a new occupational therapist, Rachel, explained to her my background, and told her I had apparently had a miracle. Rachel was excited over the news and said, "Well, lets go over here and document this miracle."

Every strength test was remarkably improved. As she tested my fingers, hands, arms, neck and shoulders, she referred to the past records lined up beside the new form she was filling in. I may not understand the results of the testing, but I know that the difference between a "2" and a "12" in finger and hand strength, and a seven-second coordination exercise that took me one minute a year ago, is a remarkable improvement. With each reading, she shook her head and commented how awesome it was. Merideth said he wanted to cry as she worked with each phase of the examination.

Then came Tina. She would check my lower body. When I arose from a chair, she said, "I saw you get up with no hands." She laughed joyfully. "Let me see if we can find anything to improve on this time."

Obviously, we couldn't. Like the occupational therapist, she reported after each phase of the evaluation.

"Just wait until the doctor sees these documents," she said. Pointing to a space on the documents reserved for recommendations and instructions to the patient, she added, "All I can do is write right here, 'Keep stretching, and enjoy yourself.'"

We were finished with the morning evaluations. I would return to see the doctor at 12:30   Merideth and I did a little shopping at a nearby mall, ate at the Pasta House, Inc., and returned to the clinic.

When I was escorted to the examination room by the volunteer, I told her what the excitement out front was about. I had been in a wheelchair fifteen years and now I walked in for the first time. "Praise the Lord!" she remarked, seating me. I was later moved to a corner room because someone with a wheelchair needed that one. I didn't notice my durable equipment representative as I walked by a group of medical people in the hallway.

When I saw who it was, I got up, walked to the door and said, "Kip, I didn't see you as I passed by. I've been intending to come over and see you, but I have been so busy for the past nine weeks." (Kip is with Southern Illinois Surgical Equipment in West Frankfort, where I got all my equipment. It was he who customized the new wheelchair for me, and he is a special representative for MDA and a therapist.)

He talked about how great I looked. Kip was full of questions, and I witnessed for my Lord with each response. He was very busy seeing other patients, so I promised I would visit him at West Frankfort to finish our discussion.

With all the other medical people, including doctors, nurses and therapists, you can imagine what went on for the next hour. The doctor was overwhelmed with my reports, and the therapists had to come in and tell him for themselves, urging him to hurry and look at what had happened since last year's evaluation, tests showed that my sedimentation rate (sed.rate) had dropped to 10. The level of sediments in the blood indicate how active the disease is. The low rate of 10 was good news, and confirmed no disease activity.

In dismay, Dr. Gardner said, "I don't know what to say." He said he knew this was real, but he would certainly like to see me again next year. I told him no problem. Heartily, he shook my hand, looked at me eye-to-eye, and said, "I can't do anything for you today. Congratulations, Rachel. I am so happy for you."

Well, what a glorious day. The reactions were all I had prayed for. I left my little indoor scooter with my MDA patient coordinator to be available for anyone who needs it.

✿ ✿ ✿ ✿ ✿

ONE YEAR LATER: OCTOBER 10, 1998:

God has opened many opportunities for me to share what Jesus means to me. Merideth and I still wake up praising Him through the wee hours of the morning. His favorite comment is, "I'm still mystified!"

Throughout the year we have visited many churches, homes, and other gatherings. We have seen lives changed and some people healed. Our church is full of joy and we still pray for the power of the Holy Spirit to do mighty things in the midst of His church. Our families are amazed that I am no longer weak and confined to the wheelchair. People in the town of Johnston City still talk about it.

The medical community has been most receptive. I have spent hours with medical professionals (doctors, nurses, heart surgeons, and other medical staff members) answering their sincere questions as simply as I can. While some of them admit at first that they are skeptical, after seeing me and hearing what Jesus has done for me, they join me in my excitement.

Heart surgeon, Dr. Eeric Thompson of Springfield, Illinois, said, "I have heard healing stories of which I have been skeptical, but I believe you. You are credible." Then he shook my hand, wished me well and said, "Keep on telling that story, and when your book is finished, I want to be the first to read it."

The response has been overwhelming. I have many letters, notes, and e-mail messages from people who have been encouraged and healed since they heard my testimony. What I desire most is to show and tell who Jesus is.

A niece from Texas said to me as I was leaving a family reunion, "Thank you Aunt Rae for showing us who Jesus really is."

🌿 🌿 🌿 🌿 🌿

Update As of November 18, 1998

As I promised last year, I returned to the MDA clinic for a scheduled evaluation. Therapists' examinations that morning showed no sign of muscular dystrophy. Each agreed that there was nothing more they could do for me. I would see Dr. Gardner at 1:00 o'clock, and it would be up to him to discharge me.

In the afternoon there was an atmosphere of celebration. I had my camera with me prepared for a photo session. Dr. Gardner, the MDA nurse, the MDA patient coordinator, and two therapists pleasantly posed for it. Each took a booklet of my testimony and offered their assistance in getting this book published.

Dr. Gardner wanted to know if he did anything to get me out of the chair. I told him no, it was the Lord. But I assured him that he was there for me with his skills, and I appreciated that. He chuckled as he explained to me why he asked such a question. If he did anything, he wanted to know what it was so he could help his other patients. I told him he could help them by telling them about the ultimate healer, Jesus. Then I offered him my two-part booklet.

He graciously took it and said, "Let's get some pictures for your book."

After the photo session I said, "Well, am I discharged from MDA?"

"You're discharged!" replied Dr. Gardner. "I'll make my report."

To be released from being one of Jerry's Kids after seventeen years was a dream come true. I will always be grateful for Dr. Gardner and those who worked with me since 1982, when I first became one of Jerry's Kids. In my travels I have transferred from one MDA clinic to another. Each doctor and medical team has ministered to me with loving care. I have seen God at work through these people.

Some of us may wait fifteen years for our ultimate healing, but God's grace is sufficient. My story is simple. I was lame and now I walk. Opportunities to witness to His saving and healing power come daily from Him. The joy of the Lord is my strength.

After her miracle, Rachel no longer needed this specially modified wheelchair.

"Congratulations, Rachel," says neurologist Dr. Robert Gardner, you are discharged from the MDA (Muscular Dystrophy Association Clinic). "I'm happy for you."

Dr. Gardner, who directs the MDA Clinic, and Tina Abate, the clinic's physical therapist, were among the medical experts who verified Rachel's healing.

Together with Dr. Gardner, Lori Dobbs, patient coordinator for MDA, (left) and Deborah Drury, an MDA nursing specialist, (right) were part of the team.

To order additional copies of

RISE UP &
WALK!

A JOURNEY TO HEALING

send $12.99 plus $3.95 shipping and handling to

Books Etc.
PO Box 4888
Seattle, WA 98104

or have your credit card ready and call

(800) 917-BOOK